THE BEST OF THE HIGHLANDS

Compiled by Douglas Gunn

Introduction

The Best of the Highlands is a book devoted to that part of the 'auld country' around Fort William. So, having defined the area in general terms, I am sure that a few eyebrows will be raised by the choice of such a title and these eyebrows will be elevated both by some native Scots and regular visitors alike because, in their mind's eye, they will picture their own favourite corner of this beautiful and hospitable land which they would rate for such a title. Now any such opinion of a region must necessarily be a subjective one. So why the title? The region in Scotland covered by this book is the district of Lochaber with its capital Fort William and some of those districts immediately surrounding it. The extent of the area is outlined on the back cover. It embraces rugged mountain grandeur including the massive Ben Nevis, beautiful glens with long fresh-water lochs lying peacefully at their foot or some with sparkling rivers dancing throughout their length. There are deep sea lochs on the west of the area which drive their shafts deeply into the mainland, a dramatic coastline, an abundance of wildlife and to accompany all this it is steeped in the richness of Scotland's historical heritage. It is sometimes referred to as the 'land of the bens, the glens and the heroes' and sometimes it is called 'Prince Charlie's land' and well may it lay claim to both of these titles. At the heart of the region is that area known in historical times as Lochaber which lies at the southern end of the great glen between the hills north of Loch Arkaig in the north, Loch Leven in the south, Loch Treig in the east and Glenfinnan in the west. Lying to the north and west of old Lochaber are those wild romantic areas of Knoydart, Morar, Moidart, Ardnamurchan, Morvern, Sunart and Ardgour – what names to conjure with.

Since regionalisation in Scotland in 1975, the present Lochaber district includes all of these areas, thus stretching the new Lochaber boundaries right out to the west coast. This all adds up to a land which is unsurpassed in Britain for its sheer scenic splendour. As you travel around the area, many breath-taking landscapes will be unveiled to you and I hope you will be able to learn a little about, and perhaps be sensitive to, the land's history – some of it bloody and some of it romantic. One of the many historical events closely connected with this area and the most widely known is the second Jacobite rising of 1745. It was here among its rugged hills and glens that Prince Charlie raised his Standard to rally the clans and set out on his moving but ill-

Looking across Bishop's Bay, Loch Leven, to the Glencoe mountains

fated quest for the crown of his fathers. Though the venture was finally crushed at Culloden the following year it was without doubt the greatest campaign in the history of the clans. Not only did the story start here but after it had run its course it also ended here. In this territory the hunted Prince was protected and sheltered by his loyal clans until he could be spirited away to the Outer Isles and thence to the Isle of Skye by the faithful Flora MacDonald and finally to France and a life of exile. It is a striking reflection of those times that despite the facts that so many Highlanders were slain in battle, many brought to ruin and their lands wrested from them, and with a price of some £30,000 on his head – a fortune in those days – no one betrayed their Prince.

I believe that anybody visiting Scotland, despite the obvious enjoyment of the visual scene, will enhance their stay if they can appreciate to some extent the historical background of the region in which they travel. Perhaps the finest and most satisfactory way to enjoy any region is to digest the local history and while doing so savour it in all its seasonal moods and then preferably on foot. But of course few of us can set aside the time required for such an appreciation in depth. So here we have aimed at achieving as much of this objective as possible in the belief that most visitors will be using a vehicle of some sort to travel around. In an attempt to simplify the pleasurable task of seeing and appreciating as much of the region as possible, we have divided the region into five geographical areas with a map at the start of each section illustrating the extent of each area. In a further attempt to avoid possible confusion we have adopted, with their helpful co-operation, the same areas as defined by the Fort William and Lochaber Tourist Organisation. They are:

1. Glencoe and Loch Leven
2. North Argyll
3. Road to the Isles
4. Fort William and Ben Nevis
5. Glen Spean and the Great Glen

Each map shows the communications and the places of interest in that particular area and indeed shows without defining it in detail what may be considered as a practical route to travel around the area. It is not always possible or desirable to complete a circular route without overlapping into an adjacent area and sometimes it is easier to radiate from a central point but this will be apparent from an examination of each map. For each area there are notes on places of interest, including historical notes, placed in the order in which we encounter them as we proceed around the suggested route leaving plenty of scope for diversions.

In Part 2 of the book there are notes on a number of specific topics of more general interest which we hope will add a little more to the reader's enjoyment and thereby enhance his stay in Lochaber.

Part 3 is devoted entirely to the everyday needs of visitors. It is a ready reference covering many items including such things as accommodation, food, amenities, things to do, sports, what's on, useful telephone numbers, shopping, travel, etc. – all designed to simplify life for the visitor and make his or her stay in Lochaber all the more enjoyable.

Glencoe and Loch Leven

This area is popular with visitors for very obvious reasons: it is easily accessible, being on one of the main routes up from the south and east; it has a wide range of facilities to cater for many interests; it has that unchanging mantle of a beautiful Highland glen; and the perpetual interest of history abounds. Glencoe, which runs through the heart of the area, is largely under the custodianship of the National Trust for Scotland or the Forestry Commission, and vies with many other candidates for a place at the top of the list of beautiful Highland glens. If your first approach to Glencoe is from the east, you will enter the glen after coming across Rannoch Moor and dropping down to the floor of the glen, with the magnificent craggy bluff of Stob Dearg (3,345 feet) ahead of you on your left and on your right the Kings House Hotel, which lays claim to being the oldest inn in Scotland. A few miles after crossing the bridge over River Etive you will pass through the gorge and the dramatic mountainscape of the Three Sisters of Glencoe, Beinn Fhada, Gearr Aonach and Aonach Dubh tower in the front of you. It was in this beautiful glen that the treacherous murder of the MacDonalds took place at the hands of the Campbells led by Campbell of Glenlyon. Though this was a remote part of the Highlands in those days, the infamous deed aroused the anger and shame of almost the entire nation – not only the act itself, which was bad enough, but the treachery involved.

Glencoe has been developing its skiing facilities over the past few years and this includes a chair-lift and ski-tows at White Corries about a mile and a half from the Kings House Hotel. The ski-lift which is normally used for access takes skiers 850 feet up the mountain to an altitude of 2,090 feet and further T-bar tows rise to an altitude of 3,600 feet. Because the selection of the sites of the ski-slopes took account of local drifting habits, the depth and state of the snow is consistently good for skiing. Even the most fervent advocate of Scottish skiing would never claim that the weather competed with Alpine weather – but the skiing is good.

At the head of Loch Leven is another example of the introduction of industry into what would be considered a remote Highland glen. At the turn of the century the village of Kinlochleven did not exist, but in 1904 work was started on an aluminium works powered by a hydro-electric scheme from the Blackwater reservoir, in the mountains to the east of the loch, and the village sprang up around the works. Although the works are dwarfed by the surrounding beauty and when you are at a distance from the village they merge into the general scene, when you are close to it the works strike a discordant note. However, they are of high social value to this Highland region and this fact must not be forgotten.

This whole area is a paradise for climbers and walkers.

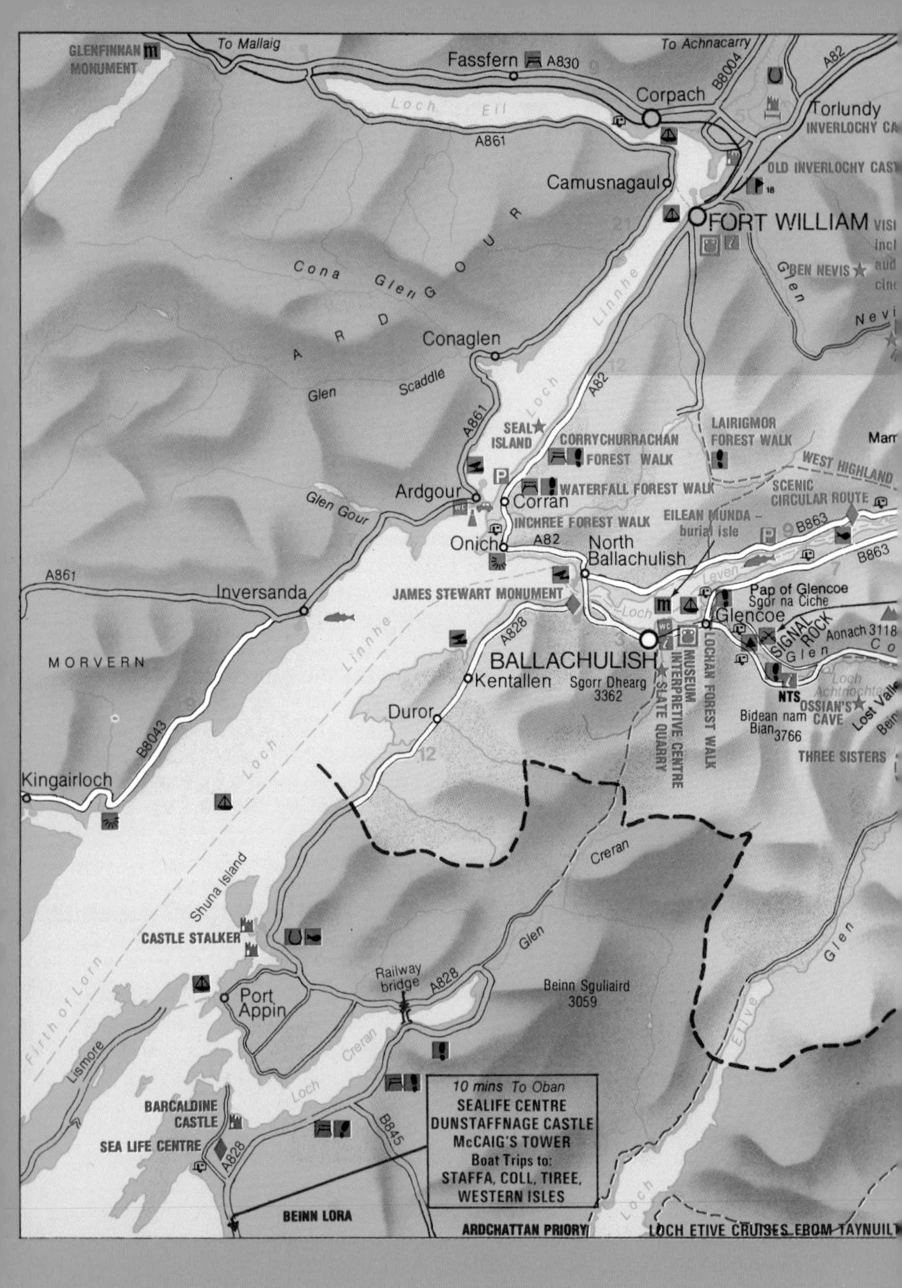

Glencoe and Loch Leven

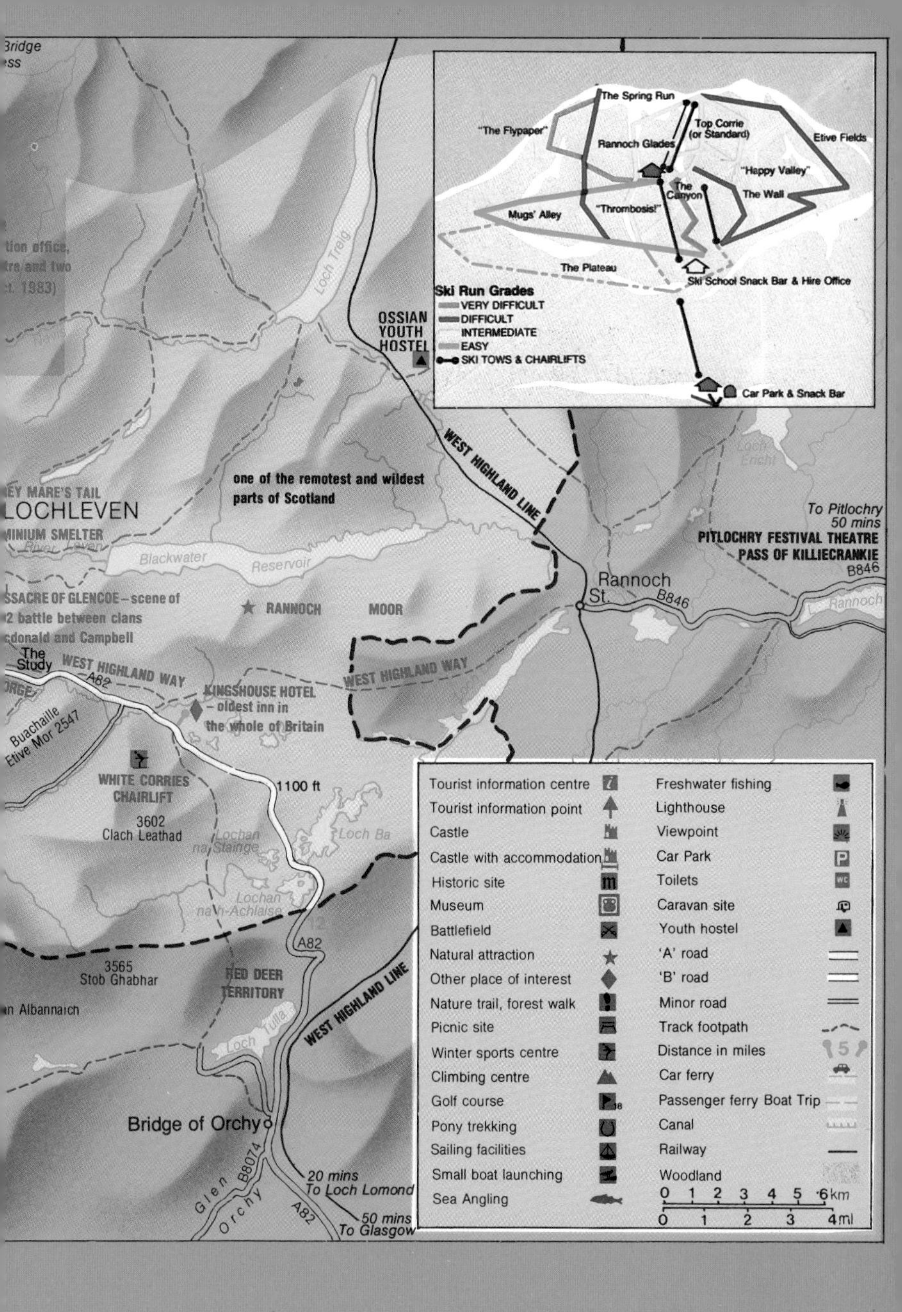
The Spring Run
"The Flypaper"
Top Corrie (or Standard)
Rannoch Glades
Etive Fields
"Happy Valley"
The Canyon
The Wall
Mugs' Alley
"Thrombosis!"
The Plateau
Ski School Snack Bar & Hire Office
Ski Run Grades
VERY DIFFICULT
DIFFICULT
INTERMEDIATE
EASY
SKI TOWS & CHAIRLIFTS
Car Park & Snack Bar
Loch Treig
OSSIAN YOUTH HOSTEL
WEST HIGHLAND LINE
one of the remotest and wildest parts of Scotland
LOCHLEVEN
Blackwater Reservoir
Loch Ericht
To Pitlochry 50 mins
PITLOCHRY FESTIVAL THEATRE
PASS OF KILLIECRANKIE
B846
Rannoch St.
RANNOCH MOOR
WEST HIGHLAND WAY
The Study
A82
KINGSHOUSE HOTEL – oldest inn in the whole of Britain
Buachaille Etive Mor 2547
WHITE CORRIES CHAIRLIFT
1100 ft
3602 Clach Leathad
Lochan na Stainge
Loch Ba
Lochan na h-Achlaise
3565 Stob Ghabhar
RED DEER TERRITORY
Loch Tulla
Bridge of Orchy
Glen Orchy
B8074
20 mins To Loch Lomond
50 mins To Glasgow
Tourist information centre
Tourist information point
Castle
Castle with accommodation
Historic site
Museum
Battlefield
Natural attraction
Other place of interest
Nature trail, forest walk
Picnic site
Winter sports centre
Climbing centre
Golf course
Pony trekking
Sailing facilities
Small boat launching
Sea Angling
Freshwater fishing
Lighthouse
Viewpoint
Car Park
Toilets
Caravan site
Youth hostel
'A' road
'B' road
Minor road
Track footpath
Distance in miles
Car ferry
Passenger ferry Boat Trip
Canal
Railway
Woodland
0 1 2 3 4 5 6 km
0 1 2 3 4 ml

Corran

This village stands on the east side of Loch Linnhe at the narrows which take their name from the hamlet. It is from here that the ferry plies its way across that narrow neck of water to Ardgour, saving a drive of some forty miles round the head of Loch Eil. Remembering that Loch Linnhe is tidal, the Corran Narrows are subject to very strong currents at certain states of the tide. There is a great deal of pathos in the story of an old Highland woman who had been wrenched from her home by the Clearances and was about to be shipped overseas with her family. When she was asked if she was not afraid to sail over the ocean to America she responded that if they managed the passage through the Corran Narrows safely then they had little more to fear. Nowadays with modern propulsion methods, they present no real hazard to shipping but in the days of sailing ships this was quite another matter. During the '45 rising naval vessels making for Fort William in adverse weather conditions were frequently ambushed in the narrows by clansmen firing on them from the shore. Ultimately the Government cleared the shores on both sides by burning the trees and flattening all buildings in order to deny cover to any Jacobite sniper.

Onich

Just a little over a mile south of Corran the road bends eastwards, when it comes to the wide inlet in Loch Linnhe which leads to the entrance to Loch Leven. Just where the road changes direction is the village of Onich which is really an extension of North Ballachulish. The noted Gaelic scholar Dr Alexander Stewart, better known by his pen name 'Nether Lochaber', was the parish minister here for fifty years from 1851 to 1901. He was responsible for the translation of many Gaelic works into the English tongue and was also one of the founders of the Mod, an annual event to foster

The view across Loch Linnhe towards the mountains of Ardgour, at the Corran Narrows

Gaelic poetry and song which is roughly comparable to the Eisteddfod in Wales. A monument, erected in his memory by his many friends in the form of a large Celtic cross, stands in the old burial ground of Innis a' Birlinn about three-quarters of a mile north of the Corran ferry.

In a field near the loch is an ancient standing stone which bears the name **Clach a' Charra**. This monolith stands about seven feet high, is perforated by two circular holes, and is of unusual shape. Like the many standing stones in Scotland the age of Clach a' Charra is judged to be about 4,000 years. Will the mystery ever be unravelled as to the origin and meaning of these standing stones?

Loch Linnhe from Onich

North and South Ballachulish

Before the road bridge was opened in 1975 the two settlements of North and South Ballachulish were connected by a ferry which transported man and machine across these narrow rushing waters. Otherwise there was a detour of some eighteen miles via Kinlochleven around the head of the loch. The views from North Ballachulish are really superb. To the east across the islets of Loch Leven there is the imposing cone of the mountain known as the **Pap of Glencoe** standing sentinel over the mouth of the glen on one side, and the craggy mass of the **Three Sisters** to the south of the glen. Away to the west across Loch Linnhe you have the

Loch Leven and the Morvern mountains from above Ballachulish

rugged panorama of the Ardgour mountains which, if you are fortunate enough to view this scene at sunset, will provide you with a memory which will linger pleasantly and long. Then immediately to the south and towering over Ballachulish are the twin peaks of **Beinn Bheithir** (pronounced Vare).

South Ballachulish, which is in Appin, is an area which stretches from the bridge to Laroch some two miles to the east. This area is unique in this part of the Highlands, having experienced the impact of industrialisation during two eras. It was at Laroch that the Ballachulish slate quarries were opened as long ago as 1693 and were only finally closed down in 1955. Then at the head of the glen at Kinlochleven the large aluminium plant was opened in 1908. I will say more about the aluminium plant under Kinlochleven, but I find it remarkable that two such contrasting and quite large industrial units sprang up so close to one another in an area which, certainly in those early days, was still a remote part of the Highlands. Sadly the need for even the high quality slate produced at Ballachulish has been replaced by more modern materials and this fact rang the death knell of the quarries. It is a little difficult to imagine the place when the quarries were fully operative, during a period which spanned over 250 years. In the year 1875 there were nearly 600 men employed in the quarries. Because of their quality the slates were in great demand, fetching a price 10 to 15 per cent higher than any other Scottish, Welsh or English slate, and at about that time the quarries were producing up to seven million slates per year.

By far the most famous historical association of Ballachulish is with the **Appin Murder**. A granite monument, on a knoll on the hillside close by the road bridge, marks the spot

The Pap of Glencoe and Loch Leven

where James Stewart, or 'James of the Glen' as he was known, was hanged in November 1752 for, as the inscription records, '. . . a crime of which he was not guilty'. It is an intriguing story. Appin is Stewart country and after the '45 rising, as with other clans loyal to the Jacobite cause, the Stewart lands were confiscated. In 1752, when the murder took place, Colin Campbell of Glenure was the Government factor in Appin. He was a sworn enemy of the Stewarts and, in the years prior to the murder, 'Glenure', the territorial name by which Campbell was known, systematically evicted Stewarts from their holdings of the better land and replaced them with Campbells. On 14 May 1752 Glenure was engaged on another purge of the Stewarts in Appin. After crossing the Ballachulish ferry he set off with his party, which consisted of a servant and two court officials armed with eviction orders, along the old winding hill road round the coast through Kentallen. It was here that he was murdered, shot in the back twice by an unknown assailant who made his escape without being seen. At the time of the shooting 'James of the Glen', who himself had been evicted from his farm in Glen Duror, was sowing oats on his small-holding at Acharn and he was the first person encountered when Glenure's manservant went off to seek help. At this period of time the Stewart chiefs were in exile in France. James Stewart, now of Acharn, who was a half brother of Ardsheal, the exiled chief, was the leader of the Stewarts who remained in Appin and was outspoken in his opposition to the evictions. As an important Campbell had been murdered and the assailant had escaped, the Campbells felt the need for revenge. So James Stewart was arrested and thrown into jail where he languished until his trial on 21 September. The trial is remembered in the Highlands as the most notorious and serious case of legal injustice. Remembering that the Campbells were the instrument of the Hanoverian government, the trial took place at Inveraray, the seat of the Campbells. It was heard before the chief of the Campbells, the Duke of Argyll, who was Lord Justice General in Scotland and before a jury chosen by the Duke which included eleven Campbells. The result was inevitable, despite the fact that no clear evidence of guilt was produced. James Stewart was hanged at Ballachulish at sunset on 8 November 1752. The body was chained up and left hanging there under guard for two months and when it had been reduced to bare bones and started falling apart, the bones were wired together again and re-hung. The gibbet was not removed until late the following year. The mysterious part of the story is that it is generally accepted that the name of the real murderer was known to the leading Stewarts of Appin at the time and the secret has been handed down through the generations, remaining a family secret to this day. As the retention of such a secret allowed an innocent man to hang for a cold-blooded murder he did not commit, it is hardly likely that the secret will ever be divulged. The event was made famous by Robert Louis Stevenson in his novel *Kidnapped*, and it was he who conferred on Colin Campbell of Glenure the appellation 'the Red Fox'; he was not known by this name in real life.

Glencoe

The glen is seen at its best by approaching from the east. This would be the normal approach by visitors from the south and east, but even if you travel from the west you may well retrace your steps at a more leisurely pace to enjoy all that this famous majestic glen has to offer in the way of spectacular rugged scenery and such amenities as a National Trust for Scotland Visitors' Centre, a tourist information office, a museum, good accommodation, forest walks planned and set out by the Forestry Commission, and a chair-lift up one of the mountains. It is generally accepted that Glencoe extends from Rannoch Moor in the east to the sea at

The Three Sisters of Glencoe

Loch Leven in the west, though in truth the eastern extremity of Glencoe is about four miles west of Kings House Hotel. As you are ascending the route from the east over the last stretches of Rannoch Moor, sweeping round the buttress of the mountain **Meall a' Bhuiridh**, the dark mass of **Buchaille Etive Mor**, the Great Shepherd of Etive, which stands in the angle between Glencoe and Glen Etive, comes into view. This mountain is a popular playground for the rock climber at all times of the year. On the south of the road, opposite the Kingshouse Inn, is the White Corries chair-lift mentioned in the Introduction, which takes skiers, in the winter, and sightseers, in the summer, up Meall a' Bhuiridh.

A little way beyond the Kings House Hotel a road branches south

Below: *Rannoch Moor;* bottom: *Blackrock Cottage and Buchaille Etive Mor*

A lochan in Glen Etive

through **Glen Etive**. It is rewarding to make a diversion down the glen a matter of some ten miles until the River Etive pours its waters into Loch Etive. The top of the glen is flanked by bare mountains on each side, but it is easy to walk down to the edge of this delightful river which dances along its route by a succession of small waterfalls and deep pools until it reaches its journey's end. About half way along the glen there is the small settlement of **Dalness**. Here the glen opens out into a pleasant valley with the mountains standing further back from the river and the waterfalls are more pronounced here than at any other part of the river. The valley retains this placid character until it reaches its exit to the sea at Loch Etive. The road ends at the remains of a pier at the head of the loch and the view here is superb, with the rugged craggy Beinn Trilleachan to the west of the loch. This is another mountain which is popular with rock climbers. There is no road access along either side of the loch so any communication is on foot, pony or by boat.

Returning to Glencoe and proceeding westwards past the Great Shepherd of Etive, the road bears to the left at a group of buildings which is the small settlement of **Altnafeadh**. Here the old military road can be seen branching off and zigzagging up the hill by way of the Devil's Staircase, leading eventually to Kinlochleven. This gives a fine walk of six miles in good weather but can be more than treacherous in winter. When the Blackwater Dam was being built on the other side of the hill in 1905, before the advent of great mechanical earth-moving equipment, an army of navvies was employed on the site and many of them would make their way over the pass to spend a convivial evening at the inn at Kingshouse. Sadly, on the return journey over the 'Staircase' in winter many perished from exposure, their bodies only being found in spring when the snows melted. Shortly after Altnafeadh the route passes the Little

The Kings House Hotel, River Etive and Cron na Creise

Etive Shepherd on the south of the road and there is a track which runs along the pass between the two Shepherds to that lovely spot at Dalness in Glen Etive. Just beyond the Little Shepherd of Etive the road runs by the side of the River Coe through a deep gorge, with the waters of a tributary falling into it from quite a high waterfall and the whole plunging through the gorge to a confluence called 'Meeting of the Three Waters'. To the north of the gorge on the old road is a flat-topped rock named the Study, which is a corruption of Stiddie, the old Scots name for Anvil, and this is at the head of Glencoe. The view of Glencoe from the Study stamps on the mind's eye of the beholder the bleak, bald character of this far from typical Highland glen, with the Three Sisters of Glencoe, the corrie-scored outlying spurs of the massive Bidean nam Bian mountain, dominating the south side of the glen and the jagged ridge of the Aonach Eagach commanding the north side.

Emerging from the gorge the bed of the glen flattens out, and on the south side of the road the River Coe empties into the small Loch Achtriochtan, lying below the rocky buttress of Aonach Dubh. High on the craggy face of the rock is the narrow, dark slit of the **Cave of Ossian**, son of Fingal, and legendary Gaelic bard of the third century. The cave is only reached by a fairly difficult rock climb by way of Ossian's Ladder. Just beyond Loch Achtriochtan a secondary road branches off, which takes you to the village of Glencoe or **Carnoch** via the Clachaig Hotel by the north bank of the river. The main road keeps to the southern bank. On the bare top of a wooded knoll between the Clachaig Hotel and the river stands **Signal Rock** which is accessible from the main road via a footbridge over the river. This is the place from which the MacDonald chiefs summoned their clansmen in an emergency but it was not used by Campbell of Glenlyon to start the infamous massacre of 1692, as is sometimes stated. Carnoch, the village of Glencoe, now lies between the two roads and straggles down to the shores of Loch Leven. There are some beautiful views down the loch, looking west to the mountains of Ardgour, with the island of **Eilean Munde** set in the loch just offshore and commanding the entrance to the glen. The island is named after the saint Fintan Mundus and the ruins of his chapel can still be seen. It was burned down in 1395. The island was used as the burial place of the MacDonalds of Glencoe, the Stewarts of Ballachulish and the Camerons of Callart, the area on the north side of Loch Leven. Each of the clans had their own landing place which they used when transporting their dead to the island and suitably enough these were commonly called 'Ports of the Dead'. There are some graves on the island dating back to the fifteenth century.

In the village of Carnoch the Glencoe Folk Museum is worth a visit and on a hillock along a lane running about 100 yards upstream from the old Bridge of Coe stands a monument in the form of a tall, slender Celtic cross. This monument was erected 'In memory of MacIain, Chief of Glencoe, who fell with his people in the massacre of Glencoe'.

The Massacre of Glencoe. It is probably this treacherous event which is first recalled whenever the name of Glencoe is mentioned. It is an event which reverberated around Scotland for a century or more and is not likely ever to be forgotten. It was the premeditated pre-planned annihilation of an entire clan, connived at by those in public office and used as an instrument of government, and then the treachery under which the attempted annihilation was carried out that caused such shock waves of disgust and anger throughout Scotland. In the end these waves caused so much disturbance that they eventually forced the Government to set up a Commission of Inquiry to investigate all the circumstances surrounding the event. When considering this affair it should be remembered that at this time, towards the end of the seventeenth century, there was considerable unrest in Scotland with many of the clans divided between those who had agreed to support, and had taken an oath of allegiance to, William of Orange, who had acceded to the throne in 1688 when James VII was deposed, and those Jacobites who supported James and wished to re-establish him on the throne. It was in 1689 that the Highlanders who supported the Jacobite cause revolted under the leadership of Claverhouse, Viscount of Dundee. Though they defeated King William's Government troops at Killiecrankie, Claverhouse was killed during the battle and without his leadership the Rising was crippled. The MacDonalds of Glencoe were Jacobite supporters who had fought with Dundee at Killicrankie, whereas the Campbells, under the Earls of Argyll and Breadalbane, were supporters of William and their clansmen were Government troops. One other factor was the deep-seated enmity between the Campbells and MacDonalds which had lasted for generations.

In August 1691, William proclaimed a pardon for all the clan chiefs who had not already sworn allegiance to him if they took the oath by 1 January 1692. None of the chiefs who were loyal to the Jacobite cause were willing to sign such an oath without the permission of the exiled James, so two messengers were secretly sent to Paris to see if King James would release the chiefs from their oath of allegiance to him. This he was reluctant to do immediately, but eventually relented and on 12 December sent back the two messengers, releasing the chiefs and telling them in as many words to do what was best for the good and safety of their people. However, he had left his decision far too late to allow the messengers time to get back to Scotland and circulate the news to the numerous chiefs. One of the messengers, Duncan Menzies, made heroic efforts to recover some of the time lost through James's indecision. He reached Edinburgh from Paris on 21 December in a matter of some nine days – a remarkable feat at that period – and, though in a state of exhaustion, went on to his home in Perth which he reached the following day. Once there he was able to despatch his own trusted messengers to all the clans and most of them got to their destination in time to allow the chief to take his oath before the Sheriff, as was required by the pardon issued by William. Because of the bitter weather, Duncan Menzies' messenger did not reach Glencoe until 29 December and the old chief MacIain, with two trusty retainers, set off immediately on ponies for Fort William to swear his oath of allegiance before Colonel Hill, the Governor at Fort William. Here, Colonel Hill, who had established quite good relations with the clans, told Glencoe that the oath must be administered by the Sheriff at Inveraray and it was quite clear that it was almost impossible to reach Inveraray in time. So he wrote out a letter to the Sheriff of Argyll, Sir Colin Campbell of Ardkinglas, asking him to accept the old man's oath despite missing the deadline as was likely. MacIain set off on the sixty-mile journey to Inveraray in a blinding snowstorm, being forced to take the longer coast road as it would have been impossible to take the shorter track through the mountains. As fortune would have it they were challenged by a party of red-coated soldiers of Argyll's regiment at Barcaldine and despite Colonel Hill's letter, they were delayed there for twenty-four hours, a delay which removed any last chance of them reaching Inveraray in time. When they reached Inveraray on 1 January they found that the Sheriff was spending Hogmanay with friends and indeed did not return until 5 January. Sir Colin Campbell had a reputation for fairness and this was proved in that, although he could see no reason for accepting any excuses considering that the pardon declaration had been issued in August, he nevertheless agreed to accept the oath, late though it was, and told MacIain to call back the following day. MacIain of Glencoe swore the oath of allegiance to William on 6 January and Sir Colin Campbell despatched the sworn oath to Edinburgh with a letter of explanation, together with Colonel Hill's letter. All this was to no avail – it was not accepted.

The Secretary of State for Scotland, one of William's close advisers, was Sir John Dalrymple, the Master of Stair. The Commission of Inquiry, in 1695, disclosed that he had made plans to destroy the Clan MacDonald in Glencoe if MacIain did not sign the oath. Although he knew of Colonel Hill's letter and the late-dated oath of allegiance, it was he who used the lateness of the signing to render it invalid and provide him with the excuse to put his plan into operation. He ordered Sir Thomas Livingstone, the commander of all troops in Scotland, to destroy the clan and added 'I hope the soldiers will not trouble the Government with prisoners'. There were many other supporting documents written in the same vein, giving proof that the Government as a matter of policy planned to exterminate the whole clan. It was on 1 February that Campbell of Glenlyon, with 120 men of the Argyll Regiment, arrived in Glencoe and asked to be billeted in the glen, giving his word of honour that no harm was intended. MacIain, completely unaware that his oath of allegiance had been rejected, accepted the situation and after a few days the MacDonalds and their guests became accustomed to one another. Soon in the afternoons they were playing games together which included shinty, gaelic hockey played with a curved stick and a round stone, running, archery and wrestling, while the evenings would be spent playing cards and singing and dancing round the fires, fortified by whisky and wine brought in by the soldiers. The Campbells were in the glen for twelve days before their orders arrived. The plot was to murder the MacDonalds in the early morning before it was light and, in order to ensure none of the MacDonalds got away, other troops were to seal up all the exits from the glen. The whole exercise needed very careful timing and reasonable weather conditions if it was to be completely successful. The orders included such phrases as '. . . that none be spared nor the Government troubled with prisoners . . . put all to the sword under seventy . . . put into execution at five o'clock'.

The orders reached Glencoe late on Friday evening, 12 February, when Glenlyon was playing cards with MacIain's two sons Alasdair and John. He excused himself on a pretext, summoned his officers and gave them their orders. These were passed down the glen in secrecy from house to house and the private soldiers were only to be given their instructions at the last moment. They were roused at three o'clock. A blizzard broke out in the early hours of the morning and was still raging when at five o'clock the Campbells set upon their hosts. The old chief was murdered as he rose from his bed, his wife stripped naked and her rings forced from her fingers by a frenzied soldier's teeth. She was released to escape into the hills, bruised and shocked, and there she perished. The facts record that when

Glencoe, looking towards the Chancellor ridge

the corpses were counted later that day they numbered but thirty-eight. It was estimated that there were about 400 MacDonalds in the glen, so the planned mass annihilation obviously failed. MacIain's two sons escaped as did the majority of the clan, although an unknown number perished in the hills while trying to make their escape in the atrocious weather conditions. However, the weather factor was probably more of an advantage than a disadvantage to the MacDonalds in that it prevented the Government troops, who were to seal off the various exits from the glen, getting into position at the appointed time, so that many of the MacDonalds negotiated the high passes to the south before they were sealed off. It seems fairly clear that another saving factor was the reluctance of the Campbell private soldiers, many of whom had grown to like their hosts, to break the traditional laws of Highland hospitality, so strictly adhered to and freely given by the MacDonalds, by an act of cold-blooded murder. It is clear that many of the MacDonalds were warned and many tales have been handed down of Campbell soldiers deceiving their officers to allow their hosts an opportunity to escape. Throughout the rest of that day the houses were sacked and burned down, the cattle and sheep driven off and the glen left empty.

Dastardly deed that it was, it did not turn out to be the mass murder that was politically planned. The Commission of Inquiry eventually found Stair guilty but cleared Livingstone on the pretext that he could have assumed that the orders stemmed directly from the King. Later the same year Stair was granted a pardon by the King. The other officers involved were found guilty but the King would not allow them to return from Flanders to stand trial. Stair retired to his estates but was later reinstated while Livingstone finished with a peerage and a statue in Westminster. So all the perpetrators of this atrocity went free and unscathed. Each year on 13 February a small band of dedicated MacDonalds gather in the shadows of that slender Celtic cross by the old Bridge of Coe to hold a short service in memory of MacIain and his followers who were slaughtered on that fateful day.

The MacDonalds re-settled the glen and twice more rallied to the Stewart cause in the Jacobite risings of 1715 and 1745. The sad, ironic twist in the history of the glen is that a clan which had survived extinction by a government-planned massacre was eventually decimated in 1820 by the advent of the sheep and the resultant clearances.

Kinlochleven

At the turn of the century the area now occupied by the township was known as Kinlochbeg, south of the River Leven, and Kinlochmore, on the north side, each settlement consisting of only three houses. Then the North British Aluminium Co. decided to set up a factory on the site, to be powered by hydro-electricity. This required the construction of a dam to increase the storage capacity of the Blackwater Loch in the hills to the east, and work on both projects was carried out between 1904 and 1907. At the time the dam was built it had the largest water storage capacity in Europe – some 4,000 million cubic feet. The water from the dam runs along a roofed conduit about three and a half miles long before it falls through six thirty-nine-inch pipes one and a quarter miles long to drive the turbines in the factory power station. It is obvious that these works were completed more with a view to providing work on a larger scale than ever imagined in such a remote area of the Highlands, than to preserve the character of the countryside at the head of the loch. I am sure such aims were laudable and forgiveable but they have left a bit of a scar on the countryside, which becomes less apparent as you distance yourself from the township. However, the journey round the head of the loch is rewarding enough and as you journey back along the north shore of the loch there are some wonderful views across the sea loch to the mountains of Appin. When you are opposite the burial isle of Eilean Munde there are some excellent views up the wide entrance of Glencoe.

Callart

Just opposite the entrance to Glencoe is Callart House, which is a fairly modern replacement for the old Callart House, burnt down in the early part of the seventeenth century because of an outbreak of plague. This was carried to Callart by a Spanish ship trading in silks and satins. It anchored in Loch Leven and the family from Callart House all visited the vessel and made some purchases. That is to say all but Mary Cameron, a daughter of the laird of Callart, who had been locked in her room because she had incurred the displeasure of her father. The rest of the family, who had returned to the house after their visit to the ship, contracted the Black Plague, and were driven into isolation. A party of local people were sent to burn down the house. Mary Cameron, still locked in her room, persuaded them to delay the burning until a message could reach her sweetheart Diarmid, son and heir of Campbell of Inverawe, who answered her call and contrived her escape under cover of darkness. When they arrived at Inverawe they were not admitted, but were told that they would have to live in isolation for a month in a bothy on the side of Ben Cruachan. Before that happened, Diarmid's father insisted that they take the vows of matrimony. They completed their term of isolation and returned to Inverawe to be welcomed into the bosom of the family.

Callart House was purchased by Sir Ewen Cameron of Fassifern in 1789 and the considerable treasures of Fassifern House, on the north shore of Loch Eil, were transferred to Callart in 1837. These included a bed on which Prince Charlie slept on the third night of his march from Glenfinnan. John Cameron of Fassifern was an absent host that night, because he would have nothing to do with the Rising and had left the district before Prince Charlie arrived. It is this bed which is in the West Highland Museum at Fort William. The last direct descendant of Sir Ewen Cameron to live in Callart House died in 1955.

Kentallen

Returning across the Ballachulish bridge we turn west and then south along the coast road which leads to Appin. In a little over three miles you come to the little village of Kentallen, beautifully situated at the head of Kentallen Bay, which provides a safe anchorage for yachts and where there are some fine views across Loch Linnhe to the hills of Ardgour. A road runs from Kentallen along the west side of the bay, around the headland, to Ardsheal House, which was once the home of an important cadet family of the Stewarts of Appin.

Duror

It is here in Keil churchyard that the remains of James of the Glen were finally laid to rest. The remains, literally a collection of bones, were eventually collected from the gibbet at Ballachulish and interred at Keil. James of the Glen lived here in Duror but the house in which he lived is now an undistinguished ruin.

Portnacroish

Some six miles south of Duror the route runs through the village of Portnacroish at the seaward end of Strath Appin. Comparing photographs of this village taken at the turn of the century with the village as it is today nothing has apparently changed, other than the dress of the people and the macadam road. In the Episcopal churchyard stands a monument to commemorate the victory of the Stewarts and MacLarens over the MacDougalls and the MacFarlanes at the Battle of Stalc, which was fought in 1468 just above the churchyard. This was a particularly bloody battle even for those days, with hundreds slain, and was one of a series in connection with the claim to the title of 'Lord of Lorn'. Just offshore, before reaching Portnacroish, is the **Isl•nd of Shuna**, which was described by a writer in the seventeenth century as a very fertile place with an abundance of fish round its shores. This is the site of the fifteenth- or sixteenth-century Castle of Shuna which is now a fairly comprehensive ruin at the south end of the island. Its history is obscure but it may have been a fortalice of one of the Lords of Lorn.

Castle Stalker

Standing dramatically on a small island in the shallow waters of Loch Laich, an inlet of Loch Linnhe just off Portnacroish, is the much photographed Castle Stalker, once the seat of the Stewarts of Appin. It is a simple but massive rectangular keep built in the fifteenth century by Duncan Stewart, son of the first chief of Appin. As a reward for his part in the campaign against the Lord of the Isles, this Duncan Stewart was made Chamberlain of the Isles by James IV and it is believed that the King hunted from this castle. The old name, Castle Stalcair, meaning 'Castle of the Falconer', probably stems from this circumstance. As was normal in castles of this type, entrance was by means of a ladder at first-floor level but this has been replaced by a permanent stairway. Dugald, the ninth chief of Appin, was forced to sell the estate in 1765 and from that date the castle gradually fell to ruin. Happily it has now been restored by a private owner.

Port Appin

This is reached by a road running back west from the main road about a mile south-east of Portnacroish. It is a delightful, peaceful spot with beautiful seascapes and pleasant walks along and above the coast of Loch Linnhe. Here there is a regular passenger-ferry service to the **Island of Lismore**, which, situated as it is in the middle of Loch Linnhe, provides a grandstand view of the mountain and coastal scenery all round it. It is a fertile island which accords with the belief that it derived its name from the Gaelic for 'Great Garden'. Its inhabitants were converted to Christianity in the sixth century by St Moluag, who was of Pictish association and not of the community of Irish Celtic saints. When the Scottish Episcopate was established, the diocese of Argyll located its cathedral on Lismore in the thirteenth century and thus the island was once of some importance and influence in church affairs. Sadly there is little trace remaining of this small cathedral.

Castle Stalker

Loch Creran

Barcaldine Castle

Barcaldine

Still proceeding southwards, the road takes you round Loch Creran and on the south side of the loch is the township of Barcaldine in the Barcaldine Forest, which is now owned by the Forestry Commission. As is the case with so many of the Forestry Commission forests, there are a number of well-planned forest walks. A few miles south-west of Barcaldine, by the shore of Loch Creran, is **Barcaldine Castle**, built by Sir Duncan Campbell of Glenorchy in the sixteenth century with some additions at a later period. The banqueting hall on the first floor measures thirty-seven feet by nineteen feet. It fell into a ruinous state in the nineteenth century but happily it was restored by a later Sir Duncan Campbell of Barcaldine, the work being completed in 1910. It is possible to drive to the castle where there are some superb views across Loch Creran.

North Argyll

This area includes those regions with the romantic sounding names of Ardgour, Moidart, Ardnamurchan, Morvern and Sunart. In this area you are never far from the sea or a sea loch and the region is almost encircled with water. In the territory shown by our map the coastline of sea and sea loch measures more than 300 miles, without including all the small indentations and the smaller islands, and this where the ground measures some forty-four miles by twenty-eight miles. This was the northern part of the ancient kingdom of Dalriada, which flourished from the early part of the sixth century until the middle of the ninth century and whose capital was further south at Dunadd just north of Lochgilphead. It was to this kingdom that St Columba came with his devoted band of followers and settled in that now hallowed island of Iona, just off the south-west coast of Mull. It was from this island that the concept of a unified Scotland originated and in particular we owe the name of our land to St Columba and his band of Irish Christians.

As you can see from a glance at the map, communications are sparse and the roads are mainly along the many miles of coastline and through a few mountain passes. This is an area where wildlife abounds and where an interesting experiment was set up in 1977 to assess the viability of farming deer. It was at Strontian that lead deposits were found and mined as far back as 1722. The mining operation which included the retrieval of mica and felspar continued successfully for 150 years. However, the mines are more famous for the discovery by Sir Humphry Davy, in 1808, of the metallic element of strontium in the mineral strontianite. In the form of strontium 90, this element is present in the radioactive fallout from atomic explosions, which relationship is difficult to come to terms with when you move around this wild and beautiful part of the country.

In Ardnamurchan at the headland of the same name you can stand on the most westerly point on the mainland of Great Britain. Ardnamurchan Point is twenty-five miles further west than Land's End and the views across the sea to the Hebrides, to Coll and to the Small Isles are truly magnificent. As is the case with all these western seascapes, if seen when the sun is going down the views are quite memorable and if seen from the lighthouse even more so. Any visit to the lighthouse is at the discretion of the head lighthousekeeper.

This is the territory of the MacDonalds and their kindred clans and at one time in their history their power rivalled and indeed threatened the power of the Scottish king. There are many sites in the area to remind us of those far off heady and often barbarous days of the Lordship of the Isles and the clashes with the piratical Norsemen for this title and the power that went with it. This remote region, apart from Moidart, is one which was not visited by Prince Charlie.

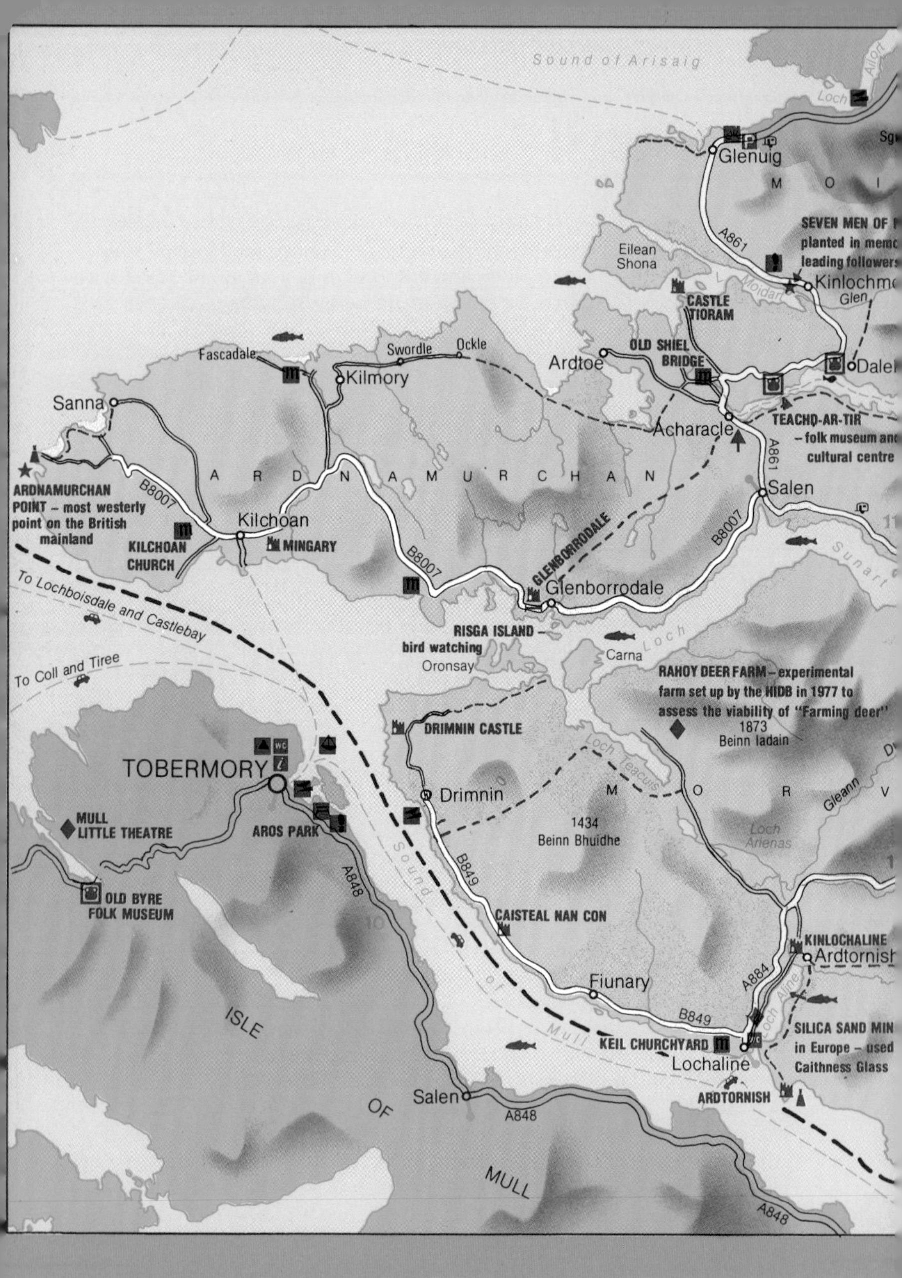

North Argyll

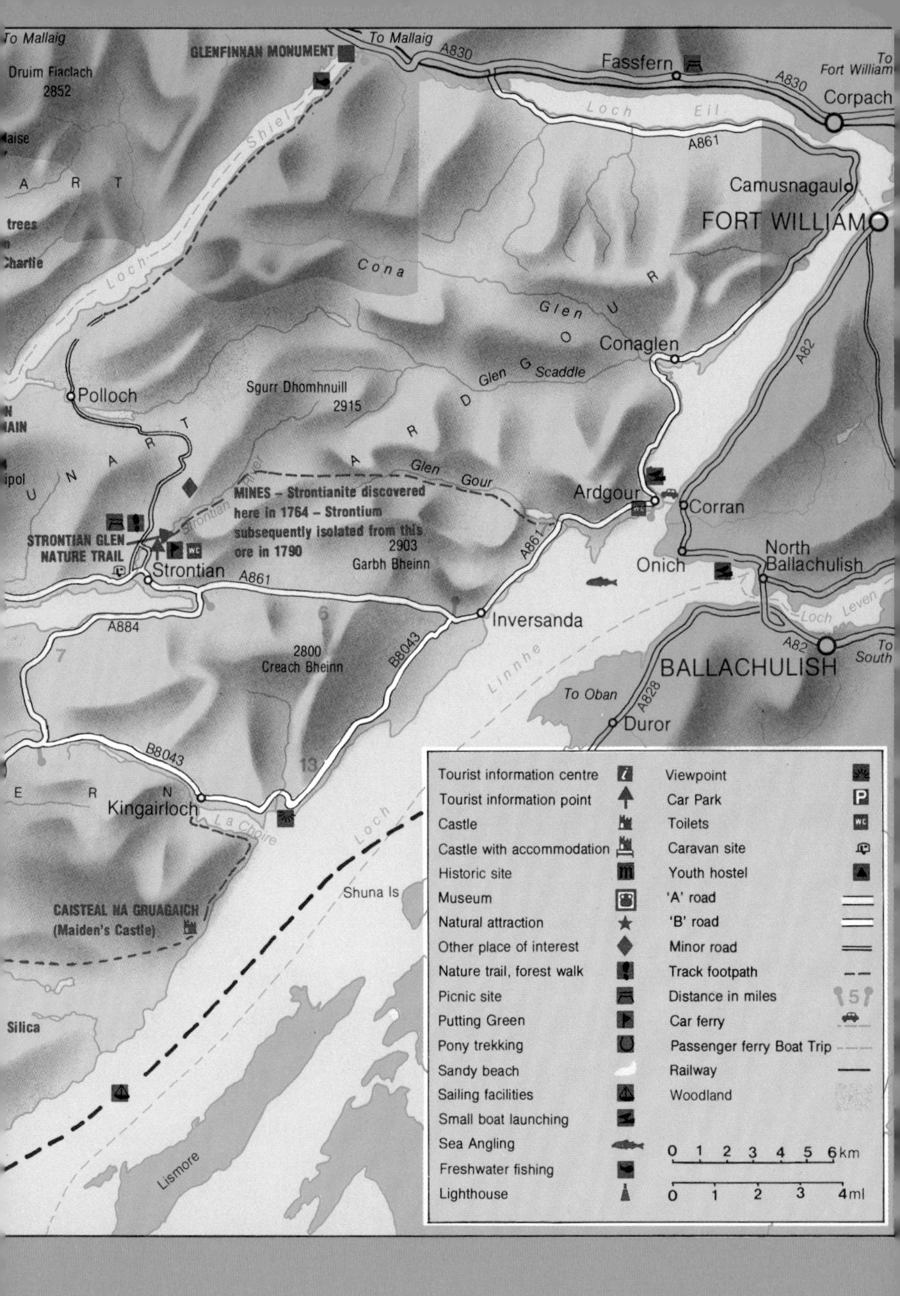
To Mallaig
GLENFINNAN MONUMENT
To Mallaig
A830
Fassfern
To Fort William
A830
Corpach
Druim Fiaclach
2852
Loch Shiel
Loch Eil
A861
Camusnagaul
FORT WILLIAM
Cona
Glen
ARDGOUR
Conaglen
Glen Scaddle
A82
Polloch
Sgurr Dhomhnuill
2915
SUNART
Glen Gour
MINES – Strontianite discovered here in 1764 – Strontium subsequently isolated from this ore in 1790
2903
Garbh Bheinn
Ardgour
Corran
STRONTIAN GLEN NATURE TRAIL
Strontian
A861
North Ballachulish
Onich
Loch Leven
A884
Inversanda
B8043
2800
Creach Bheinn
A82
To South
BALLACHULISH
Linnhe
To Oban
A828
Duror
B8043
MORVERN
Kingairloch
La Choire
Loch
Shuna Is
CAISTEAL NA GRUAGAICH
(Maiden's Castle)
Silica
Lismore
Tourist information centre
Tourist information point
Castle
Castle with accommodation
Historic site
Museum
Natural attraction
Other place of interest
Nature trail, forest walk
Picnic site
Putting Green
Pony trekking
Sandy beach
Sailing facilities
Small boat launching
Sea Angling
Freshwater fishing
Lighthouse
Viewpoint
Car Park
Toilets
Caravan site
Youth hostel
'A' road
'B' road
Minor road
Track footpath
Distance in miles
Car ferry
Passenger ferry Boat Trip
Railway
Woodland
0 1 2 3 4 5 6 km
0 1 2 3 4 ml

Camusnagaul

To reach Ardgour to set off on our exploration of North-West Argyll we can follow the first part of our 'Road to the Isles' route along the north shore of Loch Eil via Corpach and when we reach the head of the loch we turn south and then bear east along the southern shore of Loch Eil until we are opposite Corpach once more. Then the road turns south along the western shore of Loch Linnhe. Immediately opposite Fort William we come to the village of Camusnagaul which can also be reached by a passenger-only ferry from Fort William. In the Fort William and Lochaber section I describe the incredible forced march of Montrose's army before he routed the numerically superior army of Argyll at Inverlochy. During that historic battle Campbell of Argyll fled the field and left the conduct of the battle to Campbell of Auchenbreck. It was here at Camusnagaul that Argyll had anchored his galley and he was rowed across Loch Linnhe to the safety of his ship while half his army was slaughtered. Nowadays Camusnagaul still offers a good anchorage for fishing and sailing boats.

Ardgour

Proceeding south from Camusnagaul in about six miles the road sweeps round the shallow Inverscaddle Bay and in three more miles you reach the village of Ardgour, just as the road winds round the headland which reaches out eastwards to restrict the waters of Loch Linnhe at the Corran narrows. Coming from Fort William, if you do not take the long scenic route around the head of Loch Eil via Camusnagaul, the more direct route to Ardgour is by the regular vehicular ferry service across the Corran straits. Mention is made of Corran

Corpach: view of Ben Nevis from the War Memorial

Loch Eil

in the Glencoe and Loch Leven section. The narrows are guarded by the squat, white-washed lighthouse on the Ardgour side of the channel.

Ardgour is also the name of the mountainous district to the west of Loch Linnhe, stretching as far as the long, narrow, fresh-water Loch Shiel on the borders of Moidart, which name is recalled in relation to Prince Charlie and the raising of the Standard for the 1745 rising at Glenfinnan at the northern end of the loch. From the road south of the village there are some fine views to the east over Loch Linnhe to the Appin mountains of Beinn a' Bheithir and Bidean nam Bian. The road turns inland at Inversanda and shortly afterwards a lesser road branches south. After a few miles it comes out on the coast of Loch Linnhe running down to Kingairloch, and then via Loch Uisge to Lochaline. The other road also takes the traveller to Lochaline but via the less demanding route through Glen Tarbert, which brings one to the head of the remarkably beautiful Loch Sunart. Here the road divides, one branch proceeding along the northern shore to Strontian and beyond while the other keeps to the southern shore, turns south and meets up with the other route via Kingairloch and leads to Lochaline.

Larachbeg

Just before reaching Ardtornish at the head of Loch Aline, the route passes through the settlement of Larachbeg. When the people of the remote westerly group of isles of St Kilda were evacuated in 1930, because of a lack of manpower to eke out even a bare existence, Larachbeg was chosen as the place where it was believed the islanders could be rehabilitated. They were housed and given jobs as forestry workers. Sadly, this sincere effort at rehabilitation failed. The islanders, steeped in a closely knit communal way of life for generations, could not adapt to the foreign ways of the mainland. Some simply pined away and died, others drifted away to other parts of Scotland while some even tried to return to St Kilda. In the space of some forty years only one family from the islands remained at Larachbeg.

Kinlochaline Castle, Ardtornish

At the head of Loch Aline standing on a rocky outcrop is Kinlochaline Castle. The siting of the castle is not only functional but beautiful. It is a substantial ruin with some unique features. It was partly restored in 1890 by the owner of the Ardtornish Estate, Valentine Smith, which accounts for its present good state of repair. The high parapet has window embrasures rather than the normal crenellations. Here, too, unusually placed in the embattlements, is a small fireplace ostensibly for heating water or oil before pouring it down through the machicolations on to any attackers. On the ground floor it has one of those all too common dungeons with the only access via a trap-door in its roof. These grim prisons were called oubliettes for the very reason that many prisoners so incarcerated were conveniently forgotten. The date of the castle is a little uncertain but it goes back to at least the fifteenth century and it was the seat of the chiefs of the Clan MacInnes. Its history is not one of impregnability; it was breached and put to the flame by Colkitto, one of Montrose's brilliant young lieutenants, in 1644 and Cromwell's troops repeated the indignity a few years later.

Ardtornish House, the mansion house in which the landowner, Valentine Smith, and his family spent their summers, lies across the River Aline behind the castle. Another name connected with Ardtornish House is that of John Buchan, the famous novelist who spent many holidays here in the 1930s. The road to the house also leads, in about five miles along the eastern shore of the loch, to Ardtornish Castle sited on a promontory jutting out into the Sound of Mull.

Ardtornish Castle

This was one of the strongholds of the Lords of the Isles built in the fourteenth century by John, the first Lord. The castle features prominently in Sir Walter Scott's *Lord of the Isles* but his description of the buildings within is purely fictional. It is a large rectangular simple keep, a design common to the castles of that period. John, the first Lord of the Isles, died here in 1380 and his remains were interred in Iona with a ceremony of great splendour. It was here in 1461 that negotiations took place between emissaries of Edward IV of England and the Lord of the Isles against the King of Scots which eventually led to the forfeiture of the Lordship of the Isles in 1493. Looking south-east from Lochaline along the Sound of Mull conjures up a vivid picture of the defence of the territories on either side of that important waterway in days gone by, with Ardtornish Castle on the mainland and Duart Castle on the Isle of Mull, some miles away on the other side of the sound.

Lochaline

From Kinlochaline Castle the road runs parallel to the western shore of Loch Aline but high above it, and as the road descends to the village another road branches off to the west leading to Drimnin. About half a mile along this road is **Keil Churchyard** with a commanding view over the Sound of Mull. The church is dedicated to St Columba and standing close by the church is a nine-foot-high Celtic cross of the fifteenth century which originally came from Iona. Also in the churchyard is the ruin of a pre-Reformation church and close to it are a number of ancient gravestones on which there are some interesting carvings. One such carving is believed to be one of the earliest portrayals of the wearing of the kilt. It is also believed that a Spanish princess from one of the galleons that sailed up the west coast of Scotland is buried here.

Lochaline is famous for its white sandstone deposits which became an important factor during the Second World War, when, imports having ceased, it was required for the manufacture of high grade optical glass. Though hardly designed to improve the landscape the extraction, which process is virtually mining, of the various grades of sand used in the manufacture of other types of glass provides much needed employment and goes some way to stop the depopulation of an already sparsely populated region. But nobody would claim that it enhanced the beauty of this naturally beautiful area. The sandstone is now used in the manufacture of the world-known Caithness Glass. Lochaline has car-ferry services to Fishnish on Mull, directly across the Sound. It also has services to Craignure on Mull and to Oban.

Drimnin

The route to Drimnin takes you past a number of deserted settlements including Fiunary, the one-time home of the MacLeod family of Gaelic ministers. When the Rev. George MacLeod was honoured for the founding of the Iona Community in 1938 he took the name Fiunary in his title, becoming Lord MacLeod of Fiunary. A few miles further on, standing on a promontory jutting out into the Sound nearly opposite Aros Castle in Mull, is **Killundine Castle** or 'Casteal nan Con', the 'Castle of the Dogs'. It is a comparatively recent structure, built in the seventeenth century by Allan MacLean, the Killundine tacksman, and it was used as a hunting lodge by the MacLeans from Aros Castle in Mull. There is a very fine view of Tobermory from the pier at Drimnin and it is here that the road ends. But there is a track to a small deserted Roman Catholic chapel, built by Sir Charles Gordon in 1838 on the site of Drimnin Castle which once guarded the northern entrance to the Sound of Mull. Only fragments of the foundations of the castle remain.

Strontian

We return to the head of Loch Sunart, rejoin the road which came through Glen Tarbert and turn west along it into Strontian. The village lies snugly in the glen at the mouth of the Strontian river and after crossing the river there is another road which branches off up the valley through some crofting settlements and then on through moorland country until you reach some of the disused mineshafts of the old lead-mines. At the time when lead-mines were most active they employed some 500 men and the annual output was around 400 tons of lead ore. There has been some interest recently in reopening the mines and certain surveys have taken place to study the feasibility of such a proposal. The road continues for about a mile, climbing up the hill beyond the mines, and then drops dramatically some 1,100 feet in one and a half miles

Loch Sunart at Strontian

in a motor-rally-type course to Loch Doilet – not a road for the faint-hearted. The reward is some magnificent views along the route – at least for the passengers. Alternatively, one can park one's car near the lead-mines and walk to the top of the watershed and enjoy the views looking over the western slopes.

The name of Strontian was notable in a context other than the lead-mining and the discovery of strontium. At the National Assembly of the Church of Scotland in 1843 there was a bitter division of the clergy when they were considering how to deal with the thorny question of lay patronage, which had been imposed on the Church by Westminster as far back as 1712. The outcome of that bitter meeting was that 450 ministers walked out of the Assembly and thereafter resolved to form the Free Church of Scotland. It should be remembered that in doing so they had sacrificed their right to live in the manses attached to the churches, and they were left with no means of livelihood. However, the Scottish people generally upheld such a move and they rallied round and supported the ministers who had shown such courage. It was after this disruption that the minister of Strontian and his followers wished to build a church of their own, but the local landowner, who himself was a staunch Episcopalian, refused to offer any piece of ground on which they could build their new Free Church. However, undeterred the minister and his followers purchased a ship and anchored it in Ardnastang Bay about a mile to the west of the village and in

this floating church they worshipped from 1846 until 1873 when they finally won their local battle and the Free Church as it exists today was built on land near Ardnastang Bay.

Salen

The drive along the north shore of the beautiful Loch Sunart is truly memorable. The shore line is indented with many bays and there are numerous offshore islands. The village itself is beautifully situated on the wooded shore of quite a deep bay and attracts visitors in search of quietude and fishing. The origin of the village is believed to have come about when a mill was established by a Paisley mill owner but unfortunately the mill was burnt to the ground and it was only the village that remained. Here the road divides, one branch going north to Acharacle and the other branch going west to Ardnamurchan, and we will take this branch first. This village of Salen should not be confused with the village of the same name on the north coast of Mull opposite Fiunary.

Glenborrodale

The road along the north shore to Glenborrodale must be one of the most attractive drives in this part of the country, though indeed it is narrow and twisting, and when you get close to Glenborrodale the road is lined by a mile-long array of rhododendrons. There are many islands offshore which are natural breeding grounds for many sea birds. The **Island of Risga**, well out in the sound off Glenborrodale Bay, is noteworthy because some unusual cup markings have been found in its rocks. It is believed that these particular markings could have been a part of a luni-solar calendar used in times before the recording of history. The present **Glenborrodale Castle**, now an hotel, is a relatively new building constructed at the turn of the century by the Laird of Ardnamurchan. The castle was built on the site of an earlier castle whose name was Caisteal Breac (speckled castle), and this ancient castle is believed to have been a Viking watch-tower.

Cladh Chiarain, Ardslignish

When the road reaches the promontory of Ardslignish it bends to the north to avoid the mountain Ben Hiant, which means the Holy Mountain and which impedes progress along the coast. Where the road turns north it is possible to catch a glimpse of the very attractive bay of **Camus nan Geal**. There is a layby as you approach the bay and a track leads down to the shore. The beach is backed by a green field and in the centre of this field is the very ancient monument **Cladh Chiarain**, which is dedicated to the memory of St Ciaran who died in Ireland in the year 548. It is believed that the Ardnamurchan monument was dedicated by St Columba himself. The monument consists of a tall stone pillar of a red-coloured stone which bears the carving of a large cross surmounted by the carving of a dog.

Kilchoan and Mingary Castle

The road from the coast passes through moorland which strengthens the belief that this must be one of the loneliest stretches of road in the country. After a few miles you come to Loch Mudie to the east of the road and a mile beyond the loch a branch road goes off to Kilmory, while the main road descends to Kilchoan. Just before one reaches Kilchoan a track leads off southwards to Mingary Castle, which is situated right by the shore of the loch.

Although there are no precise records of when the castle was built, there is no question that it is one of the early castles of the Western Isles.

Lochan on the road to Ardnamurchan

The similarities in construction to those ancient castles of Duart and Dunstaffnage indicate that the construction was about the thirteenth century. The shape of the castle is irregular in that it was obviously built to conform to the natural configuration of the rocky site. The main entrance was in the south wall to give access to the ships which in those days were the main means of communication throughout the islands. The ditch which separates the castle from the mainland was hewn out to improve the defence capability from the landward side.

The history of the castle is a chequered one and surprisingly, despite the strength of its defensive position, it has succumbed to attack on a number of occasions. For a long period the castle was a stronghold of the MacIains, a branch of the great Clan MacDonald who were descended from the Lord of the Isles. In the tempestuous times of the seventeenth century the castle succumbed to that brilliant lieutenant of Montrose's army Colkitto, in 1644, and was subsequently used by him as a prison for a number of covenanters. Before Colkitto's escapades the castle had been captured by the Campbells in 1524. When this occurred the MacIains fled and a number of them took refuge in a remote cave on the north side of the Ardnamurchan peninsula. The story goes that their tracks in the snow were easily read by the Campbells who pursued them, and then lit a huge fire at the mouth of the cave and thereby suffocated them. This is reminiscent of the massacre of the islanders of Eigg in the cave of Francis by the MacLeods of Dunvegan in Skye, which story is mentioned under the section on the 'Road to the Isles'. Earlier still the castle was twice occupied by King James IV, in 1493 and 1495, when he was engaged in controlling the isles and it was here that he came to receive the submission of the rebel Highland chieftains. One other incident which is worth recalling is that in 1588 the MacLeans of Duart procured the assistance of 100 Spaniards from a galleon which was lying at Tobermory and besieged the castle for three days, but in this case it was without success. It was this incident which gave rise to the name of the local bay which is called the Bay of the Spaniards.

From the village of Kilchoan there is an access road which runs south to the pier from which there is a passenger-ferry service to Tobermory.

The old parish church at Kilchoan dates back to 1763 when it was erected by the Laird of that time. It provides one of the few existing examples of a 'Laird's loft or gallery'. This gallery is adjoined by a number of apartments with very old items of furniture including some plush-covered chairs which are believed to have been brought from France. There are two alternative theories concerning these chairs. One is that they were brought from St Helena and were part of Napoleon's suite and the other theory is that they were made from materials salvaged from one of the wrecked Spanish Armada vessels.

Sanna and Ardnamurchan Point

Continuing westwards from Kilchoan the route takes you to Sanna Bay. At the north end of the bay is the site of a crofting community which was established after the crofters were evicted from the more fertile area of Swordle just east of Kilmory, further along the coast. The bay itself is a delightful spot carpeted by brilliant white shell sand. To reach

Ardnamurchan Point you branch off the Sanna road about a mile from it and this road takes you to within 300 yards of the lighthouse itself. These last 300 yards are traversed on foot and visitors are allowed up the lighthouse every day at the discretion of the head lighthousekeeper. Although the view from the rocky headland is impressive enough, the climb up the lighthouse is well worth it for the higher vantage point. The tower itself is the oldest part of the lighthouse being more than 140 years old, which by coincidence is the same number of stone steps inside the tower.

Ardtoe

Acharacle and Ardtoe

Returning to Salen and striking north, the route in a few miles comes to the western end of **Loch Shiel** and the scattered community of Acharacle, which is a good centre for some really excellent fishing in the area. Before the road crosses the River Shiel by the new bridge there is a branch road going off to Ardtoe, which towards its end winds along the shores of Kentra Bay finishing up at the old pier. The road continues beyond the pier to the old settlement of Ardtoe, which is the centre of an experiment by the White Fish Authority in the breeding of sea fish. Early experiments concentrated on plaice and were not very successful, but the experiment continues. From the high ground around the bay at Ardtoe there are some fine views of the Small Isles. The sheltered beach consists of a number of sandy coves reaching in to the rocky coastline.

Castle Tioram and Loch Moidart

Shiel Bridge and Castle Tioram

Returning to the main road and turning northwards the route takes you over Shiel Bridge into **Moidart**, which heralds your return to country which was associated with Prince Charlie and the Jacobite cause. Immediately over the bridge there is a branch road which takes you to Dorlin, on Loch Moidart, and a little further north, standing just offshore, is Castle Tioram. The castle perches on the rocky summit of a tidal island and is superbly set in the midst of wooded hills and scattered islands. It is quite easily reached when the tide has receded. This is the ancient seat of the MacDonalds of Clan Ranald, which sprang from Ranald, the second son of Amy MacRuari who was the wife of John, the seventh Lord of the Isles. In order that he might marry Margaret, the daughter of King Robert II, John divorced Amy MacRuari and it was to this castle that she came with her dispossessed family. It was she who added the keep and other fourteenth-century work to what was a rude thirteenth-century castle. The castle was deeply involved in the tempestuous history involving the Clan Ranald division of the great MacDonald clan. The castle was never subdued by siege. It was, however, occupied for a short time by Campbell of Argyll who, after harrying the castle with a fleet of galleons for some five weeks, feinted withdrawal and when the MacDonalds left the castle the Argylls came back and occupied it. However, Clan Ranald had sent out the fiery cross to summon the whole clan and he returned to drive out the Campbells, not one of whom survived. The castle finally was put to the flame by Allan Dearg, the last of the Clan Ranalds to live here, when he went off to support the Jacobite rising of 1715. He correctly assumed that if he perished in that Rising the castle would have been taken over by Campbell of Argyll and rather than that he preferred to set it afire. Although it remains a ruin it is in a reasonable state of repair.

Dalelia

Returning to the main road and continuing along it for a few miles to the north-east the road branches off to Dalelia. It was from the pier at Dalelia that Prince Charlie set off on his trip up Loch Shiel to Glenfinnan after crossing from Kinlochmoidart by the track which runs due north from Dalelia. This same track was also used when coffins were being carried from Glenmoidart over to Loch Shiel for burial on the sacred isle of **Eilean Fhionnan**. There are numerous cairns along the route which marked the resting places for these rather grim processions. The sacred island of Eilean Fhionnan lies about a mile east of Dalelia in the narrow waters of Loch Shiel and is reached by a track along the north shore. It is to this tiny island that St Finnan came in the sixth century. His fame spread and he drew great numbers of pilgrims to the island. The present church was erected by the chief of the Clan Ranalds in the sixteenth century. The island has

Looking over Loch Moidart from near Kinlochmoidart

been used as a burial ground for the prominent people of Moidart, Sunart and Ardnamurchan from earliest times. In the eighteenth century that famous Gaelic bard Alexander MacDonald (Alasdair MacMhaighstir Alasdair), who was born in Dalelia in 1700, ran a school on the island for a number of years but the nature of his verse found no favour among the ruling clergy and he was forced to give up the project.

Kinlochmoidart

From Dalelia the road runs northward to the head of Loch Moidart and it was here at **Old Kinlochmoidart House**, once the seat of the MacDonalds, that Prince Charlie stayed for a week while putting together the plans for the Rising. Old Kinlochmoidart House suffered the same fate as so many other lands and properties belonging to Jacobite sympathisers when Cumberland's troops carried out wholesale sackings after Culloden. When the troops came to set fire to the house Kinlochmoidart's mother was lying seriously ill in bed. Notwithstanding, Cumberland's soldiers dragged her outside, set her down on the ground and made her watch the burning and sacking of her home. Just a little way beyond Kinlochmoidart, standing on a meadow by the lochside, are seven beech trees which were planted to commemorate 'the seven men of Moidart' who had accompanied the Prince when he had disembarked from France. One of the trees died and was replaced at a later date and this smaller tree is obvious to the beholder. From Kinlochmoidart the road proceeds north to Glenuig which brings us back into the region of the 'Road to the Isles'.

Glenuig

Road to the Isles

On leaving Corpach en route to Mallaig in the west, whether by road or rail, one is truly traversing terrain which can lay claim to being some of the most strikingly beautiful mountain scenery in the world. To enhance these scenes you can add the dramatic skylines of the offshore islands – the sunsets have to be seen to be believed. As the title suggests, this route takes you through that area which is most closely associated with Prince Charles and the 1745 rising. It was in this part of the country that he landed to set off on his romantic mission and it was here also that he departed the country as a hunted fugitive. You will soon come across the tall, rather stark monument at Glenfinnan with, at its crown, a solitary stone figure in Highland dress looking up the loch. This was erected in 1815 to commemorate the rallying of the clans to the Standard of Prince Charlie in 1745. By contrast, some miles to the west a small cairn near the head of Loch nan Uamh reminds us of the Prince's shattered dreams of regaining the crown of his fathers. It was here, with a price on his head, that he departed from Scotland some fourteen months later, never to return but to live the remainder of his life as an exile.

The three regions of Knoydart, Morar and Moidart were known in Gaelic as 'na Garbh Chriocnan' which means the Rough Bounds – so named because of their largely inaccessible and rough broken ground. With the advent of the coast roads in Morar and Moidart and the opening of the last part of the West Highland line, places like Mallaig, Arisaig, Morar and Glenuig can be quite easily reached by car and, apart from Glenuig, by rail also. But even today there is no easy access into the hinterland of these rugged peninsulas and in the case of Knoydart it still remains isolated and accessible only by sea. On the west coast there are some delightful bays including Morar Bay with its wide expanse of brilliant white sand.

At Mallaig, the end of the Road to the Isles, there is the fascination of seeing a busy ferry and fishing port bustling about its business, and hearing the almost unintelligible patter of the auctioneer at the fish market which is held twice weekly.

If you have the time there is an assortment of trips and cruises to the Small Isles of Eigg, Rhum, Canna and Muck from Mallaig, Arisaig and Glenuig – or you can follow Prince Charlie's travels to Skye. The Small Isles contrast the efforts of private owners to maintain the islands with a gentle mixture of tourism, crofting and the development of Highland crafts (as in Eigg, Muck and Canna), with the adoption of Rhum by a public body, the Nature Conservancy. This has the merit of maintaining a small population on all the islands and allows the public to visit them to enjoy their unique attraction.

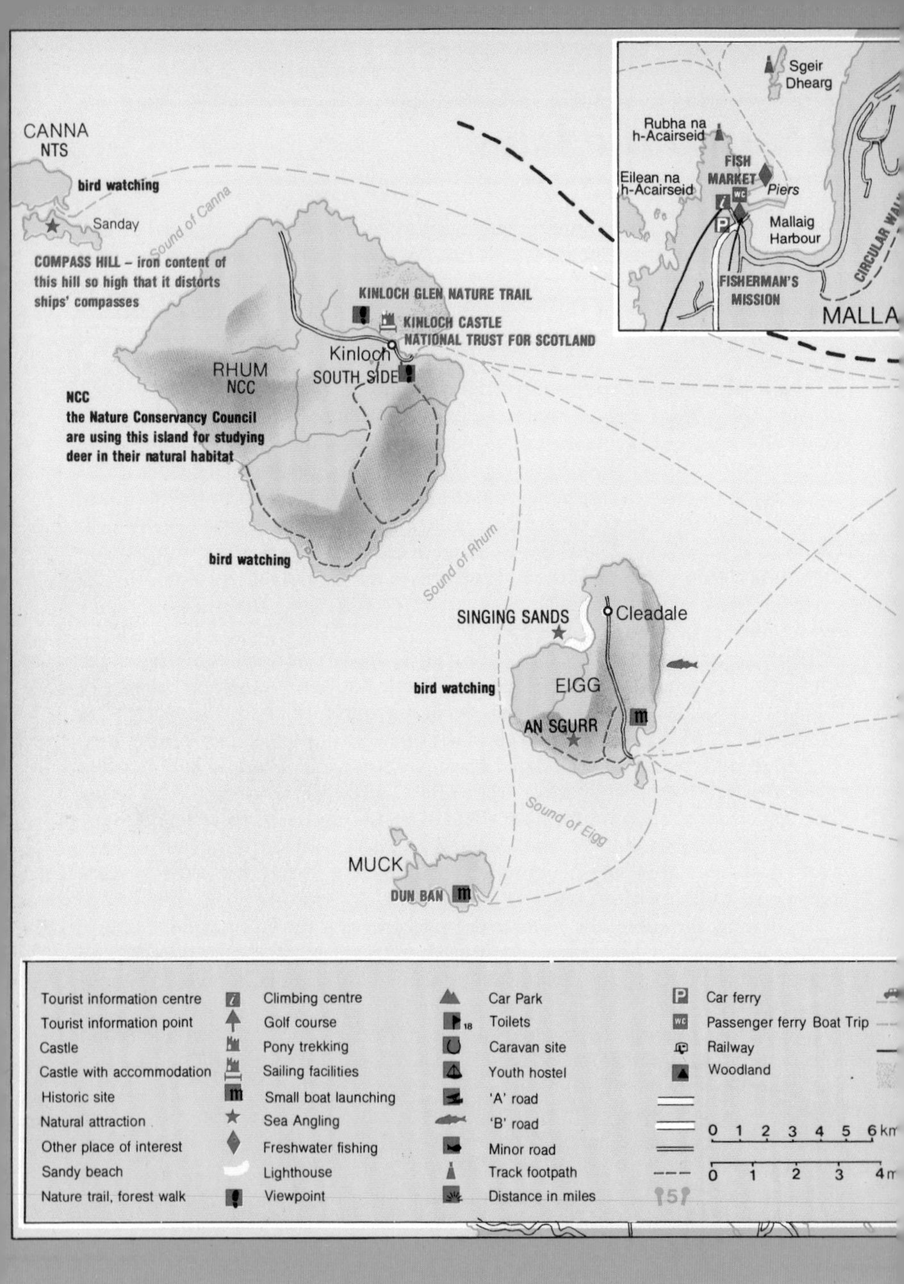

Road to the Isles

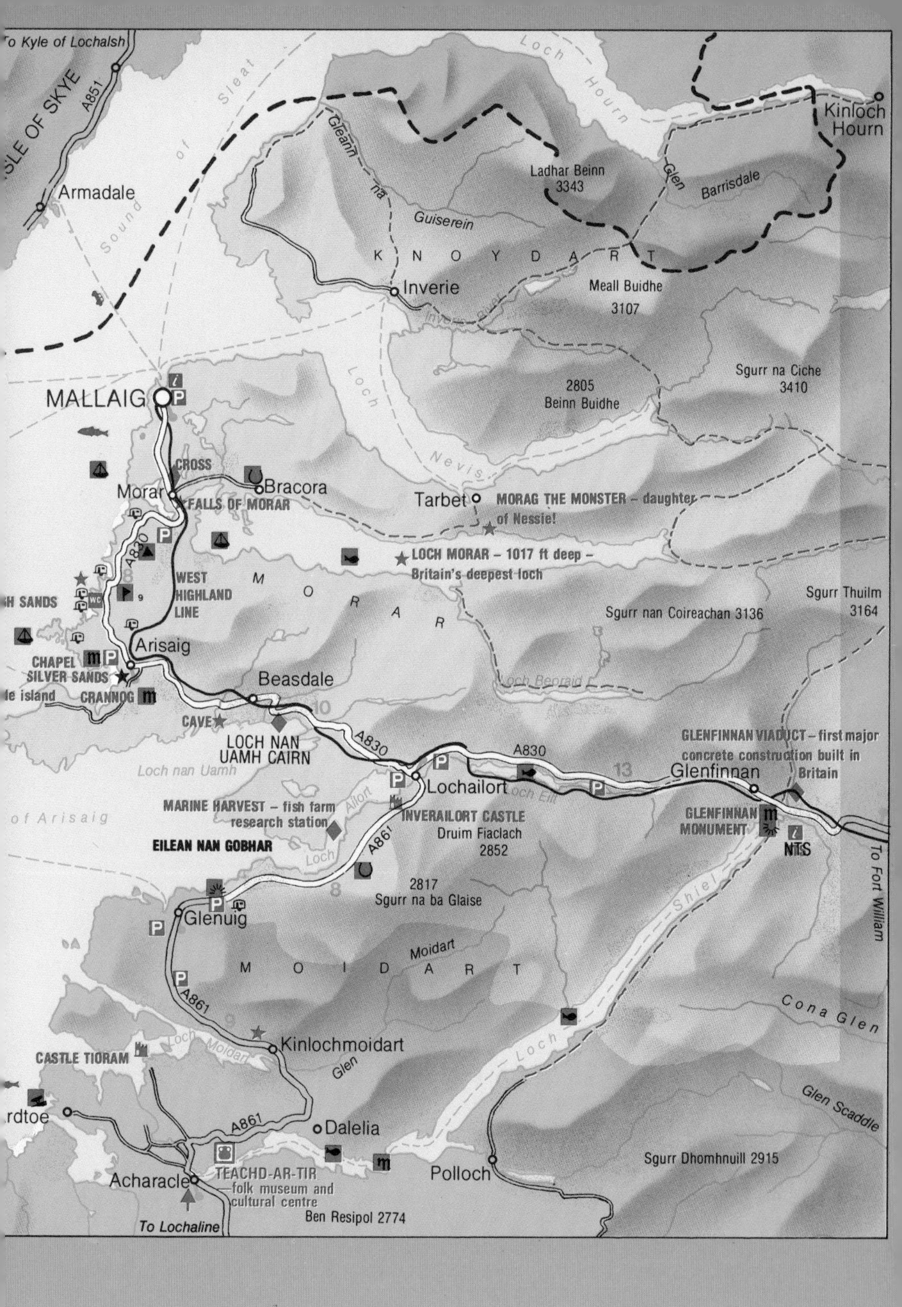

To Kyle of Lochalsh
A851
ISLE OF SKYE
Armadale
Sound of Sleat
Loch Hourn
Kinloch Hourn
Gleann na Guiserein
Ladhar Beinn 3343
Glen Barrisdale
K N O Y D A R T
Inverie
Meall Buidhe 3107
Loch Nevis
MALLAIG
2805 Beinn Buidhe
Sgurr na Ciche 3410
CROSS
Bracora
Morar
FALLS OF MORAR
Tarbet
MORAG THE MONSTER – daughter of Nessie!
A830
LOCH MORAR – 1017 ft deep – Britain's deepest loch
WEST HIGHLAND LINE
M O R A R
SH SANDS
Sgurr Thuilm 3164
Sgurr nan Coireachan 3136
Arisaig
CHAPEL
SILVER SANDS
le island
CRANNOG
Beasdale
Loch Beoraid
CAVE
LOCH NAN UAMH CAIRN
Loch nan Uamh
A830
A830
GLENFINNAN VIADUCT – first major concrete construction built in Britain
Glenfinnan
Lochailort
Loch Eilt
MARINE HARVEST – fish farm research station
INVERAILORT CASTLE
of Arisaig
Loch Ailort
Druim Fiaclach 2852
GLENFINNAN MONUMENT
NTS
EILEAN NAN GOBHAR
A861
To Fort William
2817 Sgurr na ba Glaise
Glenuig
Loch Shiel
Moidart
M O I D A R T
A861
Cona Glen
Kinlochmoidart
Loch Moidart
CASTLE TIORAM
Glen
Glen Scaddle
rdtoe
A861
Dalelia
Acharacle
TEACHD-AR-TIR – folk museum and cultural centre
Polloch
Sgurr Dhomhnuill 2915
Ben Resipol 2774
To Lochaline

Loch Shiel at Glenfinnan

Glenfinnan

On leaving Corpach the road traverses the northern shore of Loch Eil with the **West Highland Railway** following a similar route. Loch Eil is another beautiful loch and the road adheres to its northern shore for about seven miles.

About three miles beyond the head of the loch one comes to the head of Loch Shiel and there on the level ground by the shore of the loch is the **Glenfinnan Monument** which was erected by Alexander MacDonald of Glenaladale to the memory of all those clansmen who had rallied round Prince Charlie and fought for him in the '45 campaign. It is now commonly referred to as Prince Charlie's monument. The original monument, completed in 1815, included a shooting box which stood about half the height of the tower, and there was no statue on the summit. Tragically Alexander MacDonald died before the completion of the monument. One of Alexander

MacDonald's successors, Angus MacDonald, removed the two-storey shooting box leaving the tower standing on its own. At the same time he commissioned a statue of the Prince which was to be erected on the summit of the tower and this work was carried out by John Greenshields, an eminent sculptor of that time.

Greenshields called at Lee Castle in Lanarkshire not far from his own home where there hung a good portrait of Prince Charlie. Unfortunately the owners were not in occupation when he called and were not likely to return for some time. Fortunately, or perhaps unfortunately, a friend of his knew the exact location of the Prince's portrait. So, armed with this information Greenshields returned to Lee Castle and was allowed access by the staff in residence. When he located the portrait he found there were two portraits close together in the location which had been described; one portrait showed a figure in the kilt and the other one was dressed in long tartan trews. The features of both

portraits were of similar age and Greenshields assumed that the figure in the kilt was that of the Prince. So he took all his necessary measurements and sketches and proceeded with his statue. On completion he sought critical comment from the friend who had told him about the portrait and whose judgement he valued, only to find that the portrait he had used as his model was a young Jacobite, George Lockhart of Carnworth, who indeed had loyally followed and served the Prince. Greenshields refused to make another statue and never revealed his error to Angus MacDonald who had commissioned the work. However, as it was not widely known that the statue was meant to be of the Prince, no great harm was done. The statue is now in the custody of the National Trust for Scotland.

It was at Glenfinnan that the Prince landed on 19 August 1745 after being rowed up Loch Shiel from Dalelia, spending one night en route at Glenaladale. There were only a few hundred clansmen there when he landed, but it was not long before greater numbers rallied to the Standard and it was deemed that the force was large enough to set in motion the great venture. On leaving Glenfinnan the force still numbered no more than 1,200 men but the clansmen rallied round as the army advanced. By the end of August the Prince was leading some 2,000 men. After the rout of the English at Prestonpans and a few weeks' royal residence in Holyrood Palace in Edinburgh, his army had swelled to a force of 5,000 loyal Highlanders. It was this force which set out on the march south with such high expectations at the end of October 1745. It would be an insensitive Scot or any one of Scottish descent who, while standing by the

Monument at Glenfinnan

Loch Ailort

monument at the head of such a beautiful glen, was not stirred by the memory of this historic rallying of the clans at the beginning of a venture which started with such high hopes and ended so cruelly and so tragically. If you visit the monument in June or July take note of the bush bearing the lovely Jacobite White Rose – the White Cockade – which blooms so happily in this environment. The White Cockade became the emblem of the '45 rising after Prince Charlie picked a bloom from a bush at Fassifern when he stayed there on the third night of his march from Glenfinnan. The bush which blooms so profusely at Glenfinnan stemmed from a cutting of the original bush at Fassifern.

Lochailort

This settlement is situated at the head of the loch of the same name. Here the road divides, one branch going south to Glenuig and Kinlochmoidart and the other going west to Arisaig, Morar and Mallaig and we will stay with that branch of the road for the moment. It was here in Lochailort in June 1940 that a special training centre was set up to train what was then known as the Special Force. The Special Force was the forerunner of the Commandos. It was some time later that the much larger Commando Training School was set up at Achnacarry.

Loch nan Uamh

A few miles after leaving Lochailort the road to Mallaig reaches the head of the sea loch Loch nan Uamh and it was this loch that truly saw the start and finish of the '45 Jacobite rising. About half a mile past the head of the loch, standing on a rocky projection by the shore, there is a memorial cairn which marks the small bay where Prince Charlie finally em-

Memorial cairn by Loch nan Uamh

barked on 20 September 1746. The cairn was erected in 1956 by the '45 Association, now known as the 1745 Association, and National Military History Association. Shortly after Beasdale Station the road goes under the railway. About half a mile beyond this, where the road bends sharply round to the right, is the entrance to Arisaig House and just beyond that the entrance to **Borrodale House**.

It was in the little bay by the shore

at Borrodale House that Prince Charlie landed from the French Frigate *Le du Teillay* on 25 July 1745. For some days the Prince divided his time between the ship and Borrodale House where he was looked after by the MacDonalds. It was during this period that he was sounding out the various chiefs who had been summoned to meet him about the feasibility of the venture to try and reclaim his lost crown. He eventually left the ship and took up residence in Borrodale House on 4 August. Although Borrodale House belonged to MacDonald of Clanranald, he did not live there. It was one of his clansmen, Angus MacDonald, who was the Prince's host at this time. Many of the clan chiefs believed that the timing was wrong for the success of the Rising, but the Prince would not be dissuaded. Eventually he won the clan chiefs round and they promised to rally to his banner. On 11 August the Prince and his party left Borrodale House and sailed across the loch and the Sound of Arisaig to a little bay by Forsy, about a mile east of Glenuig Bay. The Prince and his party then made their way to Kinlochmoidart where they spent nearly another week before moving on to Dalelia on Loch Shiel. It was here that the Prince embarked on his journey up the loch, stopping off at Glenaladale en route for one night and then continuing to the head of the loch and the rallying of the clans at Glenfinnan.

It was here too that in a cave overlooking Borrodale Bay that the Prince hid from his pursuers after Culloden. Borrodale again features in the Prince's story when on 26 April 1746 he escaped from here to the Outer Hebrides. It was during one critical period of his wanderings in the Outer Hebrides, when it seemed inevitable that he would at last be captured in Benbecula, the small island between North and South Uist, that he made his escape to Skye. The heroic Flora MacDonald, with Lady Clanranald, arranged that the Prince should be ferried across to Skye disguised as Flora's maid. It should be remembered that the crossing of these often hostile waters was made in an open six-oared boat. It is this epic journey which is forever remembered in the Skye Boat Song. The Prince's sojourn in Skye ended when, with the net once more closing in around him, he was rowed back to Mallaig by two young McKinnons on the night of 4 July 1746. This was a long and hazardous journey of some eighteen miles in an open boat from Elgol around the point of Sleat and across the Sound of Sleat where the Government warships were scouring the sound to prevent such an escape. Success was only achieved by the selection of a stormy night, with visibility hampered by wind-driven rain. The peril of a sea crossing oared by these sturdy young McKinnons was preferable to attempting the crossing on a calmer night when the risk of interception was so much greater. The Prince landed at Mallaigvaig on the morning of 5 July, once again having successfully evaded the widely spread net of the Government forces. By this time, after his enforced privations, the Prince was lice-infested and suffering from dysentery but determined to stay free. He returned to Borrodale during July, making the trip from Mallaig over land. Then finally on 20 September he embarked from the little bay at the head of Loch nan Uamh, which is about two miles to the east of Borrodale, and was taken aboard the French frigate *L'Heureux* to be carried safely to France for a life of exile. Two of those who embarked with the Prince were Lochiel himself and Dr Archibald Cameron his brother.

Arisaig

Arisaig House

During the Second World War Arisaig House was used as the Training Headquarters for that most secret wartime organisation the S.O.E. (Special Operations Executive). These were the people who were dropped behind enemy lines to co-ordinate resistance activities and who were skilled in all the facets of underground warfare. Both Arisaig House and Borrodale House are privately owned but since March 1982 Arisaig House has been opened as an hotel.

Arisaig

Leaving Arisaig House the road winds westwards for about three miles across the neck of a peninsula which stretches some four miles into the western ocean. Although this peninsula, called Rudha Arisaig, is a very attractive place to explore it is now almost barren of habitation and communication is very difficult. Arisaig lies at the head of Loch nan Ceall, which means Loch of Small Boats, and it was so called because it was so shallow it was only suitable for small shallow draught boats. Before the opening of the road and rail links to Mallaig all communication up this coast was by sea and any stores or passengers for the area were delivered to a point at the western end of Rudha by way of a concrete jetty which can still be seen today. Just east of the old jetty is an area called Sandaig and it was in this area that Alasdair MacMhaighstir Alasdair, better known as Alexander MacDonald, the famous Gaelic poet, lived out the last years of his life.

In the village of Arisaig the Roman Catholic church, built in 1874, is quite close to the ruins of the old pre-Reformation church of Kilmory. The Reformation zeal seems to have run out near Loch Shiel and the result is that north of this line most of the inhabitants remained loyal to the old religion, as they called the Roman Catholic faith. It is in the tower of the Arisaig Catholic church that a clock was installed to the memory of Alasdair MacDonald, who is believed to be buried close to the old ruined church. It is said that he was buried here because foul weather prevented his body being taken to his ancestral burial grounds on Eilean Fhionnan on Loch Shiel. It is when the road reaches Arisaig that you get your first view of that striking panorama of the Small Isles and the Inner Hebrides, with the magical Cuillins of Skye reaching to the heavens. Arisaig is, as well as being the name of the village, also the name of the area in the hinterland.

Waterfall on the River Morar

Morar

The road from Arisaig winds its way northward and comes close to the sea in several places, sweeping round crescent-shaped bays of gleaming white sand as it proceeds northwards. Morar is famous for its white sands and the reason for the whiteness is that the sand is composed of powdered silica. Many of the other beaches of western Scotland are formed by finely powdered shells and, as a result, are more of a creamy-white colour. As with Arisaig, Morar is the name of the district and the village. As the main road crosses the River Morar before the village, there is an excellent view of the rapids of the river and the narrow waterfall. Before the damming of Loch Morar, the Morar Falls were very large and

The white sands of Morar with the Cuillin Hills of Skye in the distance

very beautiful. The village itself is at the narrow neck of land between Loch Morar and the sea and it is only a short walk eastwards from the main road to the loch. Loch Morar is some seventeen miles long and at its eastern end is easily the deepest inland water in Britain, having a depth of 1,080 feet.

At the western end of the loch there are several islands and on one of these, **Eilean Ban**, there was a Catholic seminary in the eighteenth century. This seminary was used to educate and prepare young men for the priesthood. For many years Morar was the centre for Roman Catholicism in the Highlands. After Culloden when the Highlands were being purged by Government troops, Lord Lovat and Bishop Hugh MacDonald took refuge in the seminary on Eilean Ban which was then unoccupied. All the local boats were commandeered and brought to the island in order to make their hiding place more secure and they set up a guard of some twenty clansmen. However, the commander of the

garrison at Arisaig learned of their hiding place, obtained a lifeboat from a warship lying off Arisaig, had it dragged across the narrow neck of land and sent in an armed party to arrest these eminent fugitives. Lord Lovat and the Bishop escaped in one of their own boats to the densely wooded southern shore where they successfully avoided capture at that time. The raiding party returned to the island and razed the house to the ground and from that time no one has lived on the island.

Since ancient times there have been tales handed down of a monster living in Loch Morar. In more recent times there have been more definite reports from what could be described as reliable witnesses. In August 1969, when out fishing on the loch, two reliable local men reported that the monster had risen close to them in their boat and that they had been forced to scare it off with a rifle shot. When this report was given a fair amount of publicity in the Press, other local men admitted to having seen the monster but had been hesitant to divulge this in case they were ridiculed. It has been affectionately christened Morag.

Loch Morar

Mallaig

Mallaig is quite a sizeable town and for many years it has been an important centre of the fishing industry. As such it has a very good harbour and is a busy departure point for the car ferry to the Isle of Skye. There are also regular services to the Small Isles and a variety of cruises to choose from. (Details are given in Part 3.) Sunsets from all along the western coast are usually memorable but those from around Mallaig really have to be seen to be believed. The added factor here is the dramatic silhouettes of the offshore islands of Skye, Rhum and Eigg. The road continues north for a little over a mile beyond the town to a village called **Mallaigvaig**. It was here on the morning of 5 July 1746 that Prince Charlie landed after a wild night at sea, when he was brought over from Skye by the McKinnons following his fugitive wanderings in the Outer Hebrides and Skye. At Mallaig you have come to the end of the Road to the Isles.

Glenuig

Just after leaving Lochailort on the road which branches southwards, you will see on the loch one of the fish farms of Marine Harvest Ltd, a subsidiary of Unilever. The farming of fish is rapidly becoming big business and in this particular farm they are rearing salmon. The earliest salmon are harvested at twelve months but the really big fish have to live a bit longer.

It was only in the 1960s that the

road was constructed from Lochailort to Kinlochmoidart via Glenuig. This opened up a beautiful stretch of seascape which had hitherto been accessible only on foot. Before the advent of the macadam road this was little more than a track and in ancient times was used as one of the old coffin routes. These were routes for the long Highland burial processions of past years. There were recognised stopping places along these routes and above Glenuig there are cairns and a cross signifying that this was one of them. Just at the head of Glenuig Bay there is a road on the right leading to **Samalaman**. This was the location of a Catholic seminary which was founded in 1780 as a successor to one at Buorblach on Morar Bay, which itself had been established to replace the one burned down on Eilean Ban on Loch Morar. It was later moved to Lismore, the island in Loch Linnhe near Oban, in 1804. Later still the seminary was transferred to Blair's in Aberdeen. It is believed that the Government in London encouraged such a seminary where it aimed to enlist Catholic Highlanders into the Army and so provide it with Scottish Roman Catholic chaplains who had come up through the seminary.

From Glenuig there are day cruises to the Isle of Eigg.

Mallaig harbour

The Small Isles

Four islands, **Rhum**, **Eigg**, **Muck** and **Canna** make up the parish of the Small Isles. The largest of the four islands is **Rhum** which rises dramatically from the seas with four peaks all about 2,500 feet high. After the depopulation during the clearances era the island was a private sportsmen's hunting ground with no access to the public. However, in 1957 it was acquired by the Nature Conservancy and is now used for botanical research, as well as being a centre for the study of red deer. Limited residential facilities are available by prior arrangement with the Regional Officer or Chief Warden, with priority being given to research workers, educational parties and naturalists; day visitors are welcome and there are two nature trails on the island which amply demonstrate its character. The very fine Kinloch Castle, with the panelling itself valued at some three million pounds, is open to the public but only by prior arrangement and on advertised cruise days.

Canna is the outermost of the four islands and is some twenty-five miles from the mainland. Until recently, the island was privately owned and the owner successfully saved the island from slow extinction. The island has now come into the care of the National Trust for Scotland, which plans to provide limited accommodation for visitors.

Eigg is privately owned but the owner has established ferry and light aircraft services to the mainland some eight miles away and there are a number of comfortable guest houses on the island. From the mainland Eigg has the appearance of a regular sweep of great cliffs from one end to the other but from another viewpoint there is clearly a depression which runs across the middle and it is from this depression that it has derived its name, in Gaelic Eilean Eige, which means the island of the notch. The whole island is a hill farm as indeed is the island of Muck which lies two and a half miles to the south-west. Serious attempts are being made to improve the land and the land holdings with the hope of retaining the crofting population if even on a part-time basis.

Muck is the smallest of the four islands but is quite the most fertile of the four.

The history of the islands goes back to the Bronze Age and there are exhibits of an axe head and a bronze dagger in the Edinburgh Museum of Antiquities. These were dated between 800 and 400 BC. The earliest recorded history was the landing of St Donan on the Isle of Eigg at the beginning of the seventh century AD but he and his fellow monks came to a grim end at the hands of pirates in 617. The most dominating influence in the history of the islands was undoubtedly that of the Vikings, who held sway over all of the Hebrides for some 400 years, though apart from some place-names in the Small Isles there has been little found in the way of artefacts.

The Viking domination ended after the decisive battle of Largs in 1263 and the Hebrides reverted to the Scottish crown. Then came the wild era when the Lord of the Isles dominated life in all of the Hebrides. One of the grimmest events in the history of the Isle of Eigg was the massacre in the **Cave of Francis**. The cave is situated at the eastern end of a wide rocky bay on the southernmost part of the island and is only about a mile from the jetty at Galmisdale; it is low and very large but with a small entrance. Having received warning of a raid in strength by the MacLeods of Dunvegan in Skye who arrived in a small fleet of

Sunset over Skye from Mallaig

galleys, the entire populace successfully hid in the cave until they thought they were safe. Then they sent out a scout to the top of the ridge behind the cave to reconnoitre. The MacLeods had actually given up the search and were about to leave when a keen-eyed youth spotted the scout. Unfortunately, too, there had been a light fall of snow and the MacLeods were able to trace the tracks of the scout's footsteps back to the mouth of the cave. Here they lit a great fire in the entrance and 395 people were smothered and perished.

During the time of the clearances the islanders had a temporary reprieve from the relentless evictions by the sudden need for kelp (seaweed) which was in abundance around the islands; this was needed for the making of potash for gunpowder in the war with France. However, by 1850 there was no further need for kelp and during the next few years there were wholesale evictions. On Rhum after the evictions only one family remained out of 100 families – a statistic to dwell on for a moment. Though it did nothing to erase the scars of the evictions better times were to follow. Eigg was bought by a wealthy merchant towards the end of the nineteenth century and over the years he introduced many improvements. By 1914 there were ten regular steamers per week calling at Eigg. Unfortunately the wealthy merchant, Lawrence Thomson, died in 1913. There was an easing of the improvements when his brother took over but successive owners since that time have maintained the progress started by Lawrence Thomson. He is buried on the highest point of tiny Castle Island at the south-east corner of Eigg and his grave is plainly visible as you pass the island.

The four islands are of varied interest but a visit to any one of the four is a rewarding experience.

The islands of Rhum and Eigg from near Arisaig

Fort William and Ben Nevis

As well as being the capital, Fort William is at the very heart of Lochaber. The town lies snugly on the shore of Loch Linnhe beneath the towering mass of Ben Nevis. We are concerned here with Fort William and its immediate surroundings. The town itself is a fairly obvious centre for visitors to the Lochaber region, whether they be second or third generation expatriates seeking out the lands of their forefathers or visitors with no claims of heritage in the area who are here to enjoy what this part of Scotland has to offer. The town does not live in the past but presents a superb example of the introduction of new industries to replace old ones without irrevocably disfiguring the countryside. New industries such as aluminium, paper and hydro-electric power schemes have been set up without ruining the landscape.

Glen Nevis, just a few miles from Fort William, is one of Scotland's finest glens. It is dominated by the mass of Ben Nevis, with the clear sparkling waters of the River Nevis flowing throughout its length. It is a paradise for both novice and experienced hill walkers and caters too for the expert rock climber. This is Clan Cameron country and the glen has its share of historical reminders including Glen Nevis House which was Lochiel's headquarters during the Highlanders' unsuccessful siege of Fort William in 1746.

Here, too, you can set off on the wondrous railway journey on that part of the West Highland Line which runs from Fort William to Mallaig. The rigours which must have been experienced by the construction teams while driving a railway track through the most tortuous terrain in the country during all the seasons, miles from human habitation, can only be vaguely imagined. Try to allow time to make the trip; it will be a dramatic experience of scenes which will dwell in your mind's eye for all time. During the journey of some forty miles, which takes about one and three-quarter hours, you will pass through vistas of unparalleled beauty and grandeur, seen from unique vantage points not available to the road traveller. Construction of the West Highland Line, which runs from Glasgow to Crianlarich where one part branches off to Oban and the other proceeds to Fort William and thence to Mallaig, was begun in October 1889. The 100-mile-long section between Craigendoran, some twenty miles north-west of Glasgow on the Firth of Clyde, and Fort William was opened in August 1894. The section between Fort William and Mallaig was not opened until April 1901, nearly seven years later.

Fort William itself has a comprehensive range of facilities to offer, including such things as golf, fishing, swimming, sailing, cruising, tours, tennis, and there is a Scottish Crafts Exhibition Centre, a Ben Nevis Exhibition and the West Highland Museum. Then there is a wide range of hostelries of various types where the warm welcome continues the age-old tradition of Highland hospitality.

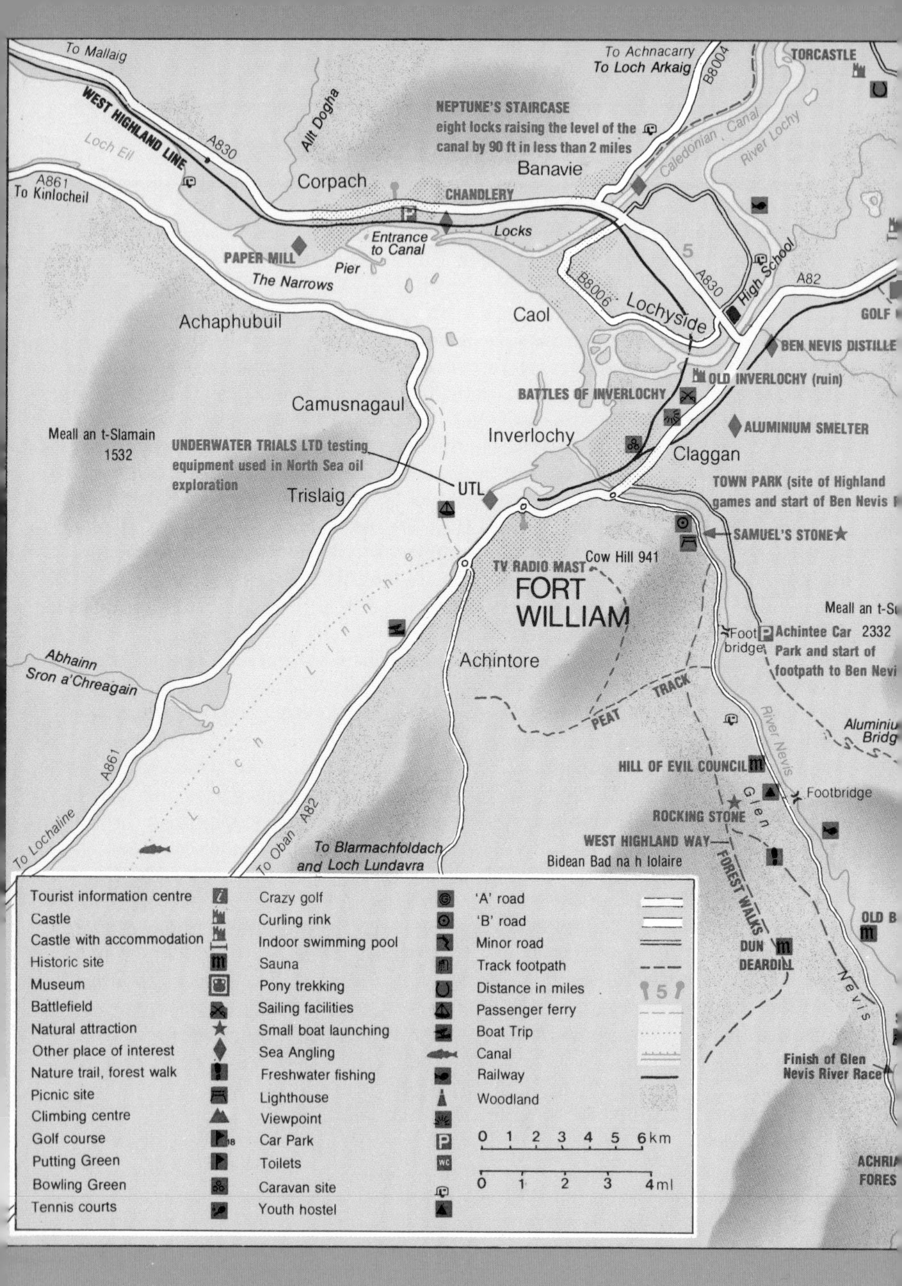

Fort William and Ben Nevis

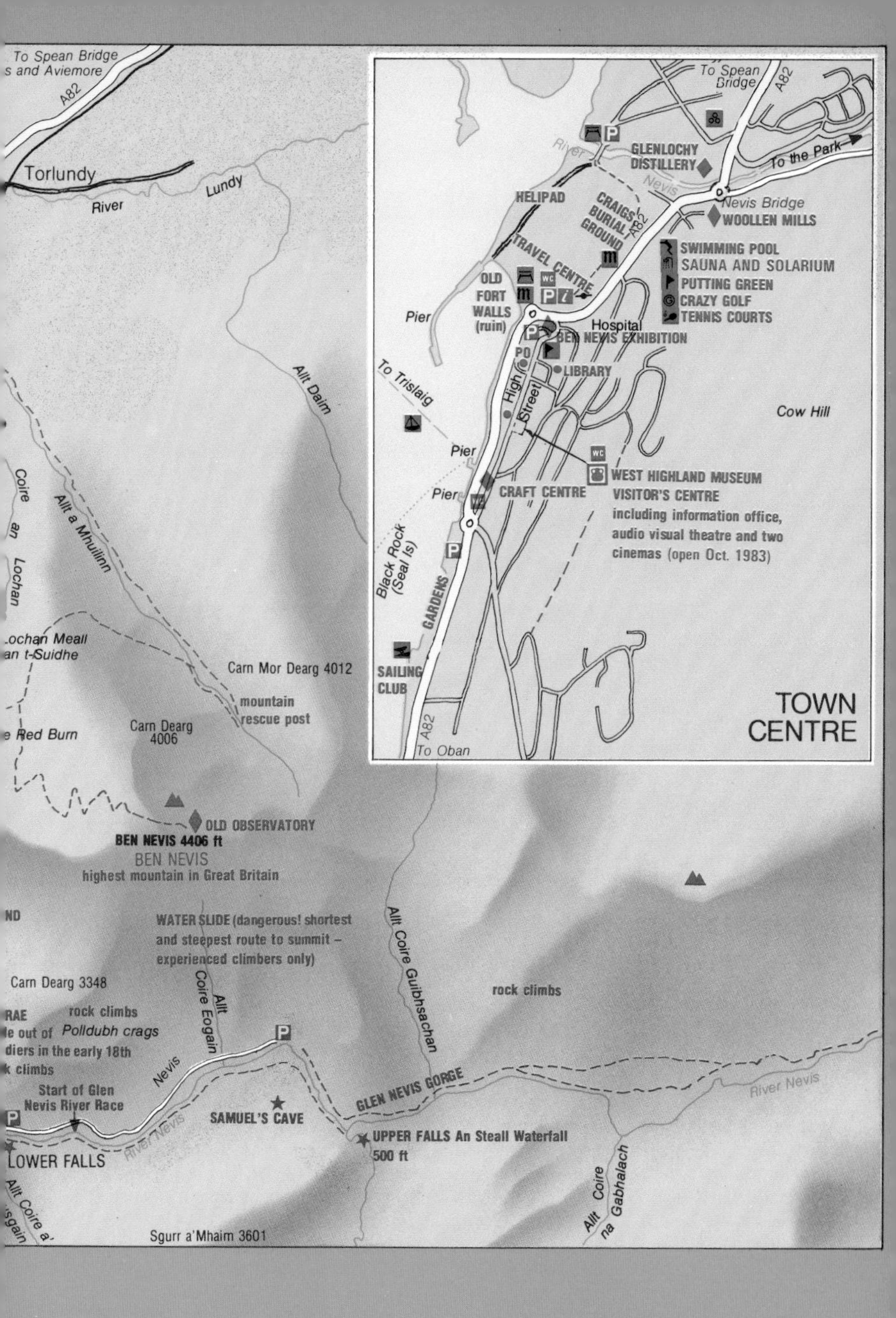

To Spean Bridge
and Aviemore
A82
Torlundy
River
Lundy
Allt Daim
Coire
an
Lochan
Allt a Mhuilinn
Carn Mor Dearg 4012
mountain
rescue post
Carn Dearg
4006
Red Burn
OLD OBSERVATORY
BEN NEVIS 4406 ft
BEN NEVIS
highest mountain in Great Britain
WATER SLIDE (dangerous! shortest
and steepest route to summit –
experienced climbers only)
Carn Dearg 3348
rock climbs
Polldubh crags
Allt
Coire Eogain
Allt Coire Guibhsachan
rock climbs
Nevis
Start of Glen
Nevis River Race
SAMUEL'S CAVE
GLEN NEVIS GORGE
River Nevis
LOWER FALLS
River Nevis
UPPER FALLS An Steall Waterfall
500 ft
Allt
Coire
na
Gabhalach
Sgurr a'Mhaim 3601
To Spean
Bridge
A82
River
GLENLOCHY
DISTILLERY
To the Park
Nevis
Nevis Bridge
WOOLLEN MILLS
HELIPAD
CRAIGS
BURIAL
GROUND
A82
TRAVEL CENTRE
SWIMMING POOL
SAUNA AND SOLARIUM
PUTTING GREEN
CRAZY GOLF
TENNIS COURTS
OLD
FORT
WALLS
(ruin)
Pier
Hospital
BEN NEVIS EXHIBITION
PO
LIBRARY
To Trislaig
High
Street
Cow Hill
Pier
WEST HIGHLAND MUSEUM
VISITOR'S CENTRE
including information office,
audio visual theatre and two
cinemas (open Oct. 1983)
Pier
CRAFT CENTRE
Black Rock
(Seal Is)
GARDENS
SAILING
CLUB
A82
To Oban
TOWN
CENTRE

Fort William

The town derives its name from the fort which was built during the seventeenth century to keep in check those clans whom Dr Johnson described as 'savage clans and roving barbarians'. The first fort, mainly a timber palisade and earthworks around the troops' houses, was built by General Monk in 1655. This was replaced in 1690 by a more substantial fort built by General Hugh McKay, who was at the time Commander of King William's troops in Scotland. It was General McKay who named Fort William in honour of his King. It was later strengthened by General Wade and this strengthened fort, with a garrison of some 600 men, held off the army of Lochiel during the siege of 1746. From the middle of the eighteenth century to the latter part of the nineteenth century the name of the settlement was successively Maryburgh, Gordonsburgh and Duncansburgh but despite these early variations the actual name of the fort has survived as the name of the present town. The fort was completely dismantled and the building sold off in 1864. In 1889 it was purchased by the West Highland Railway Company who demolished most of the remaining

Fort William and Ben Nevis from across Loch Linnhe

buildings to make room for railway sheds.

In grimmer memory Fort William was one of the Scottish ports which were used in the emigration of the Highlanders at the time of the infamous Highland clearances. Towards the end of the eighteenth century and up to the middle of the nineteenth century, many thousands of Highlanders were evicted in order to make way for sheep. They were virtually forced to leave their Highland homes because of starvation conditions. Fort William was used as a port of emigration for the people in Inverness-shire and northern Argyll as well as Lochaber. There were six other Scottish ports used in this trade in human souls. To give some idea of the scale of this monstrous eviction, in 1801 from Fort William alone eleven ships set sail carrying a human cargo of some 3,300 men, women and children. Conditions aboard the emigrant ships were nothing short of abominable. Three contractors working out of Fort William were a Major Simon Fraser, John Grant and probably the most successful in terms of trade, George Dunoon. It was said of two of Dunoon's emigrant ships which sailed in 1801 that if the laws governing slave-ships had applied to them they would not have been allowed to sail. The ships, the Sarah and the Dove, sailed from Fort William with 700 emigrants from the clan-lands of Seaforth, Fraser and Cameron packed into their tiny holds when the slave-trade laws would have limited the number to 489. As late as 1853, even after four Acts of Parliament had been passed in an effort to control and improve the dreadful conditions which prevailed in the emigrant ships, twenty-nine vessels set sail for America during the month of November of that year carrying nearly 14,000 passengers. Some 5,000 were stricken by cholera and more than 1,000 succumbed to this distressing disease.

It is not commonly known that Fort William was one of the towns in Britain which pioneered street lighting by electricity. This was achieved in 1896, and it was the first town in Britain to have both its houses and streets lit by electricity, which was generated using its own water power.

When in Fort William a visit to the **West Highland Museum** situated in Cameron Square is a 'must'. Being at the heart of Jacobite country the museum has a unique collection of mementos of the pathos and romance of that movement. But it has far more than that. It covers such subjects as local archaeology, geology, wildlife, folk exhibits and a reconstruction of the Governor's room as it was in the old fort.

At the northern end of the town on the Loch Linnhe side of the Belford Road is the **Craigs Burial Ground** which was the original cemetery for the troops of the old fort. There are many old stones in this burial ground but the most prominent monument is that erected in the middle of the nineteenth century to commemorate the Gaelic scholar and poet Euan McLachlan. (He was not buried in this cemetery but at Kilevoadain, Ardgour.) In 1843, at the time of the disruption, when one-third of the ministers and members seceded from the established Church to form the Free Church of Scotland and were refused sites on which to build their own churches, the Fort William congregation gathered to worship at the Craigs Burial Ground and seated themselves on the graves of their forebears. The arch at the entrance to the Craigs Burial Ground carries the following inscription: 'This arch was erected in 1690 over the main entrance to the Fort and re-erected here in 1896 where Sir Allan Cameron of Erracht in 1793 raised the 79th, or Cameron Highlanders, a regiment which distinguished itself on many a hard-fought field for King and Country.' The arch was originally the inner of two arches connected with a slate roof forming a gatehouse into the fort.

The remaining ruins of the fort wall can be seen on a small headland jutting out into Loch Linnhe at the northern end of the town. It lies close to the Railway and Bus Stations.

At the north end of the town close by Nevis Bridge is the **Glen Lochy whisky distillery** which was founded in 1898, and a few miles further north along the Inverness road is the **Ben Nevis distillery** which was founded as long ago as 1823. Fine malt whisky as well as grain whisky is distilled at both premises. The town itself is the shopping heart of the region and the High Street provides a variety of establishments which should satisfy the most avid shopper.

Glen Lochy distillery

Ben Nevis

It is fortunate for the visitor that, although Ben Nevis is the highest mountain in Britain and the northern side of it is extremely sheer, the ascent from the Fort William side is quite within the capabilities of anybody used to some hard walking. This has been made easier because a track was built to the former weather observatory at the mountain peak and although the observatory is no longer in use the track remains an easy path to the summit. However, extreme caution should be exercised by the inexperienced during bad weather, when it is cloudy, and during the months when the mountain is covered in snow.

The path up the mountain starts at the road end at **Achintee Farm** two miles from the village of **Claggan**. You should allow some three and a half to five hours for the ascent and one and a half to two and a half hours for the descent. The tourist path zigzags up the side of a peak called Meall an t'Suidhe to Loch Meall an t'Suidhe which is about 2,000 feet above sea level and often called 'Halfway Lochan'. Here the track divides, one section branching off to the left around to the north side of the mountain, but the main track continues in wide zigzags up the mountain following the general line of a small stream known as 'The Red Burn'. The ascent gradually gets less steep until you reach the summit plateau. Then the path skirts the edge of the main cliffs right up to the summit. On a fine day the view from the summit is breath-taking; it ranges from Ben Lomond to Torridon and from the Cairngorms to the Outer Hebrides. Possibly the most dramatic view is that across Glen Nevis to the Mamores mountains where the peaks take on the imagery of quartzite teeth.

The ruins at the summit are those of the meteorological observatory which was built in 1883 to collect data over a period of sunspot activity and it was closed down in 1904. For a time after that it was run as a hotel before the proprietor gave up the unequal struggle. Nevertheless, the records which were collected during its period of operation are of great interest to mountaineers and rock climbers but should also be borne in mind by anybody who climbs Ben Nevis. They record that there is often a cloud-cap on the summit when the rest of the sky is clear with the result that the average sunshine record per day is about two hours and the annual rainfall is 157 inches. Permanent winter snowfalls commence in October and the summit is normally clear of melting snow by July. However, the most important factor which affects everybody on the mountain is the wind and it is the combination of wind and cold which is so deadly. The summit area has an average annual total of 261 gales, many reaching hurricane force but, of course, the majority of these occur during the winter period. The lesson is that **no one should climb Ben Nevis, even by the tourist path, unless he or she is generally fit, and properly equipped with good boots, warm clothing, a map and compass, and extra food.** Remember conditions on the mountain can change dramatically and with little warning. Some relevant publications for the more serious climber to consult are given in Section 3.

Glen Nevis

To geologists Glen Nevis is a fine example of a glaciated valley. To the average visitor it is a striking example of a beautiful Highland glen which stretches for twenty two miles. To reach the glen, leave Fort William and travel north until you reach Nevis Bridge. From this point proceed straight along the southern side of the Nevis stream. Shortly after entering the glen you reach a sizeable waterfall which bears the name **Roaring Mill**, but the reason for such a name is lost in the mists of time and there is no obvious connection to either the 'roaring' or the 'mill' though the volume of water is substantial. Just beyond this waterfall there is a very large boulder which is situated on a corner of the road and which is known as **Samuel's Stone** or **Clach Shomhairle**. Folklore has it that the stone turns round on its axis three times on a certain day each year and if you are lucky enough or unlucky enough to find the stone on the move you will receive correct answers to any three questions.

A little way further up the glen, on the flat land at the foot of the hills on the right, there is an old burial ground on a small mound. The Gaelic name for this knoll means the 'Waterfall of the Shoulder' and herein lie many Camerons of Glen Nevis and other Lochaber families. In the West Highland Museum there is a 'mort safe' which was found here just before the Second World War. This is an iron coffin and it is a relic of the era of the body snatchers who were liable to break in to anything less vulnerable than an iron coffin. It is quite close to the present-day cemetery.

We next come to **Glen Nevis House** which stands in a small plantation of beech trees. It was at this house that Lochiel, supported by Keppoch, made his headquarters when with his 2,000 Highlanders he unsuccessfully laid siege to Fort William in 1746.

In a little under two miles from Glen Nevis House high above the glen on a knoll on the right is **Dun Deardui**l. This is a 'vitrified fort' which originally was built of wood, peat and stone and the whole fused together by burning. This defensive position was constructed by the inhabitants of the glen some 2,000 years ago in the Iron Age. It was thought by some archaeologists that the fusing of these forts occurred accidentally when the timberwork was set on fire by attackers. However, it is now widely believed, because these vitrified forts are found so widely, that the fusing was a deliberate technique which was used to strengthen the ramparts. A little under two miles past Dun Dearduil the road bends to the left by a farm. Shortly afterwards it crosses the river just by the picturesque **Lower Falls of Nevis** where the water gushes out of the confined channel of a rocky gorge and tumbles into a seething pool below. About a mile and a half beyond the falls the road comes to an end in a car park just after crossing a small stream called the **Water Slide**. This is the name given to several similar, unusual water descents when the water runs directly down a steep hillside without any interruption or diversion. From a distance it has the appearance of a vein of silver or quartz. The name of this stream is Allt Coire Eoghainn and it falls straight down the mountainside a matter of some 1,250 feet at an angle of about thirty-five degrees. It is sometimes referred to locally as the 'Sliding Burn'. There is a recognised route to the summit of Ben Nevis for *experienced* climbers starting up the east bank of the Water Slide.

In among the crags across the River Nevis opposite the car park is **Samuel's Cave**. In a raid by Government troops after the '45 rising Mrs Cameron of Glen Nevis House hid here with her children and a few personal maids. Having been warned of the raid Mrs Cameron, before fleeing up the glen, gathered

Waterfall in Glen Nevis

Early morning in Glen Nevis

together all the household silver and other valuables, wrapped them carefully and buried them near Glen Nevis House but away outside the garden walls and sufficiently well to avoid detection by the marauders. Enraged at being deprived of valuable loot the raiders burned and pillaged throughout the glen before they eventually found Mrs Cameron and her small band hiding in Samuel's Cave. Mrs Cameron resolutely refused to divulge the whereabouts of the hidden valuables. As she had something bulky under her plaid, which she was obviously guarding, one of the soldiers, thinking it might be some of the valuables, slit open her plaid with his knife only to find her tiny infant son. The soldier's action wounded the baby in the neck. Shortly afterwards the soldiers departed but not before stripping the women of their outer clothing. The baby survived to become laird of the glen, carrying a scar on his neck to remind him of a dastardly deed of which he had no recollection. All the party survived the ordeal and lived in the cave well into a Highland winter until it was safe to reappear.

The **West Highland Way**, which is the first 'long distance footpath' in Scotland so designated under the Countryside (Scotland) Act 1967, stretches a distance of ninety-five miles from Milngavie outside Glasgow to Fort William. The last part of the route traverses part of Glen Nevis, skirting just above Dun Deardui1 and coming out at the track opposite Achintee Farm. (See Hill Walking in Part 3.)

Inverlochy

Just north-east of Fort William and now joined to it is the village of Inverlochy which is an example of modern industrial development lying side by side with ancient historical buildings and their historical associations. The modern industrial development is the British Aluminium

Company's aluminium smelter, powered by the impressive hydro-electric scheme at Laggan. The original complex was completed in 1930 and the new, rebuilt factory was opened in 1981. The historical association is embodied in the well-preserved thirteenth-century Inverlochy Castle. The stirring history of the castle spanned three centuries from the War of Independence to the period of Montrose's brilliant campaigns culminating in an astonishing defeat of Argyll in 1645. His victory at Inverlochy, when he annihilated Argyll against odds of two to one after an incredible march via Glen Tarff, Glen Turret and Glen Roy during a very severe winter, must go down in British history as one of the most brilliant and rigorous military achievements by a fighting force. In December 1644 Montrose had carried out his famous raid on Inveraray, the seat of the Argylls, and had reached Fort Augustus in the Great Glen on his way to Inverness, which he had planned to attack. News was brought to Montrose that Argyll was hot on his tracks and had encamped at Inverlochy Castle. There seemed little doubt that Argyll intended to take Montrose in the rear. With the knowledge that there was another large hostile force ahead of him Montrose decided to double back and carry out a surprise attack on Argyll at Inverlochy. To effect surprise he had to avoid the obvious route through the Great Glen, so he led his Highlanders over snowclad mountain passes and through the rugged glens of Glen Tarff, Glen Turret and Glen Roy in the depths of a very severe winter. At the end of this forced march, he was able to rally his men and lead them to a celebrated victory against all the odds. The forced march of some thirty-eight miles was completed in two days. The actual battle took place to the south of the castle, so when you gaze on this historic ruin ponder for a moment on this tremendous feat of arms and endurance. The battle was described by Sir Walter Scott in the *Legend of Montrose*. The castle itself is a well-preserved thirteenth-century square fortress with round towers at each corner. It has two gates, one giving access to the River Lochy. There is evidence that the castle is built on the site of previous castles or defensive positions of earlier eras.

There is a modern mansion, also styled Inverlochy Castle, a mile further north on the Inverness road. This was the centre of a cattle-ranching enterprise which was established in the 1950s. Unfortunately this petered out in the mid 1970s. The castle is now an excellent but rather exclusive hotel.

Banavie

Just a little more than a mile north-west of Inverlochy we come to Banavie, lying near the southern end of the Caledonian Canal. It was here that Telford solved one of his biggest problems in the construction of the canal: to reconcile a difference of some sixty-five feet between the two water levels. He achieved this remarkable feat by the construction of eight locks in the space of about 500 yards and this superb engineering achievement is known as **Neptune's Staircase**. While at Banavie the houses of the lock-keepers are worth more than a casual glance, because they are the original buildings erected when the canal was constructed and their odd-looking bow windows were specifically designed for clear vision in both directions along the canal.

There are some magnificent views of both the Great Glen and Ben Nevis from vantage points at Banavie. It is difficult to appreciate the mass of Ben Nevis from close quarters but here one can appreciate it at its most magnificent with the massive backdrop of the mighty Monaliadth mountains fading into the distance.

Corpach

The small town of Corpach is beautifully situated overlooking the waters of Loch Eil where they meet those of Loch Linnhe. This is another place where one can behold some wonderful views of Ben Nevis. Indeed it is probably the most popular place from which to view the great mountain. This is another town which has absorbed industrial development, here in the shape of a large pulp and paper mill and a large saw mill, the largest of its type in Europe. Unfortunately the pulp mill part of the complex closed down in November 1980. The paper mill has its own port on Loch Eil. It is at Corpach that one enters the **Caledonian Canal**. Just a few hundred yards west of the Corpach Hotel stands the Kilmallie parish church. The present building is not so very old but the records of the church go way back to the thirteenth century. Just by the church there are two parish burial grounds, one of which is obviously older than the other. However, the most prominent monument, situated a little lower down than the church, is the tall slender obelisk erected in memory of Colonel John Cameron of Fassifern, who fell at the battle of Quatre Bras which took place just a few days before Waterloo.

The name of Corpach is derived from the Gaelic words 'Corp' meaning 'body' and 'ach' meaning 'place of' so that the Gaelic meaning of Corpach is 'place of the bodies'. It was so named because in past times, when the bodies of important people who had lived north of Corpach were being transported to Iona for burial on that sacred isle, they were rested at Corpach before embarkation. The same applied if any body was being transported to the ancestral burial ground of the eminent men of Moidart on Eilean Fhionnan, the Green

Neptune's Staircase, Banavie

Loch Linnhe at Corpach

Isle, on Loch Shiel. The bodies would spend one night or more here while awaiting suitable weather to transport them to their pre-destined resting place.

Lying just off the Corpach shore are four little islands named Tree Island, Lilly Island, Broom Island and the Rubha Dearg Island, the last named being closer to Caol than Corpach. The stretch of water between the shore and Tree Island is now bridged by a pipeline from the pulp mill. During the sixteenth and seventeenth centuries the Lochiel chiefs had a family residence on the island. The widow of Iain Dubh (who was the brother of Ewan the fourteenth chief) lived there with her infant son Alan. It was on this island that Alan as a child succeeded his uncle to become the sixteenth chief, and throughout his life he continued to spend a lot of his time there. It is this sixteenth chief who was the progenitor of the present head of the House of Lochiel.

Caol

This is a modern development in that it was only built after the Second World War and is a well-thought-out scheme lying on the shores of Loch Linnhe in an area which was once part of Corpach. It is considered to be the largest village in Scotland. In a population census in 1969 the population of Caol was more than the population of Fort William, both being just over 4,000. During the siege of Fort William in 1746 a Government warship twice bombarded the area occupied by the southern part of the township on the shores of Loch Eil.

Tor Castle

About two miles north of Banavie on a mound on the west bank of the River Lochy and enclosed by a loop of the river is the ruins of Tor Castle. This castle was the centre of a dispute between the MacIntoshes and Camerons which led to one of the bloodiest feuds between any of the clans in Highland history. It was a feud which was handed down from generation to generation. Tor Castle was the seat of the old MacIntosh chiefs but when they moved to Badenoch in the early part of the fourteenth century it was occupied by the Camerons who were then acting as baillies for the first Lord of the Isles. Although the MacIntoshes never relinquished claim to the title of the castle it continued to be occupied by the Camerons and indeed it remained the seat of the Cameron chiefs until they built a new castle and moved to Achnacarry in the latter half of the seventeenth century. After the '45 rising and with the departure of the Cameron chiefs the castle gradually fell into disrepair and eventually became the low ruin which it now is. The feud between the two clans was finally settled when the Camerons and the MacIntoshes confronted one another in 1665 at Achnacarry and were preparing to fight a decisive battle. A mediator in the form of Campbell of Glenorchy intervened and surprisingly achieved a peaceful settlement between the two clans. It was this agreement by which Camerons gained legal possession of the lands of Glenlui and Loch Arkaig by the payment of some £4,000 but there was a clause in the agreement which granted the MacIntosh chiefs the right to use the title 'MacIntosh of Tor Castle' which they retain to this day.

Salmon fishing on the River Lochy with Ben Nevis in the background

Glen Spean and the Great Glen

This area takes us to the northern limits of Lochaber and indeed some way beyond its accepted geographical boundaries by exploring the southern part of the Great Glen but nevertheless into an area which was much associated with Lochaber people. Glen Spean is another lovely Highland glen and the road running east from Spean Bridge, following the River Spean and by way of Loch Moy and Loch Laggan, takes the traveller to the Cairngorms, that highly developed winter sports area which still has plenty to offer the summer visitor. Spean Bridge is the site of a woollen mill which produces a fine and famous range of traditional tweeds and woollens.

The Great Glen is a geological fault which virtually splits Scotland asunder from the Firth of Lorn in the south-west to the Moray Firth in the north-east, a distance of about 100 miles. This geological fault means that in the distant past the part of Scotland north of the Great Glen was moved by some giant hand some sixty-five miles to the south-west relative to that part of Scotland to the south of the Great Glen. This has formed a magnificent wide natural corridor with a series of connecting lochs and rivers and in modern times these lochs have been connected together by means of Telford's great masterpiece, the Caledonian Canal. This enables ships of up to 150 feet long and thirty-five feet beam to sail from the west coast to the east coast of Scotland without having to travel the long, often stormy and hazardous route around the inhospitable north coast. It is truly remarkable that this tremendous feat of engineering was carried out at the beginning of the nineteenth century; Parliament passed the necessary legislation in 1803 and the canal was opened in 1822. The canal was operated more or less in its original form for a century or more and it is only in comparatively recent times that many locks on the canal were converted from manual to electro-hydraulic operation. Another great engineering achievement in this area, but of recent times, is the power supply to the great aluminium smelter at Inverlochy just outside Fort William. It starts at the great Loch Laggan dam, then the water is transported by tunnel to Loch Treig and thence by a further tunnel through Ben Nevis to Inverlochy. The north-western portion of the area is one of the remotest, most rugged and wildest parts of Scotland with little more than tracks for communication; some eight of the mountain peaks are over 3,000 feet and the whole mountainscape is laced with rivers and great inland lochs. On the edge of this wild region, on the narrow strip of land by the River Arkaig between the eastern end of Loch Arkaig and the western shore of Loch Lochy, is Achnacarry. This has been the seat of the Camerons of Lochiel since the seventeenth century, though the present house is comparatively modern being completed in 1837. Achnacarry was the headquarters of the Commandos Basic Training Centre during the Second World War and this is acknowledged on the striking monument at Spean Bridge to those Commandos who fell during that war.

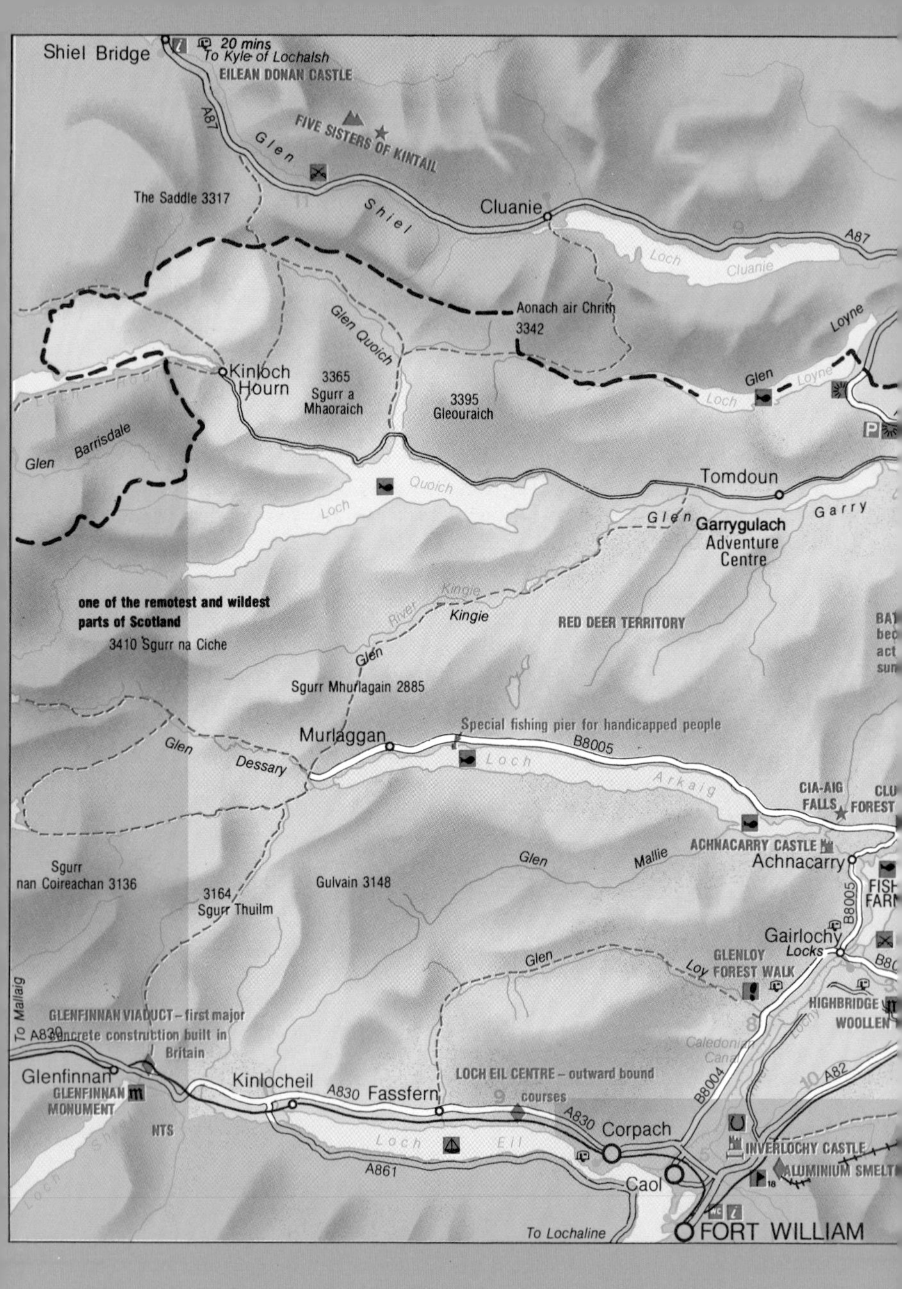

Glen Spean and the Great Glen

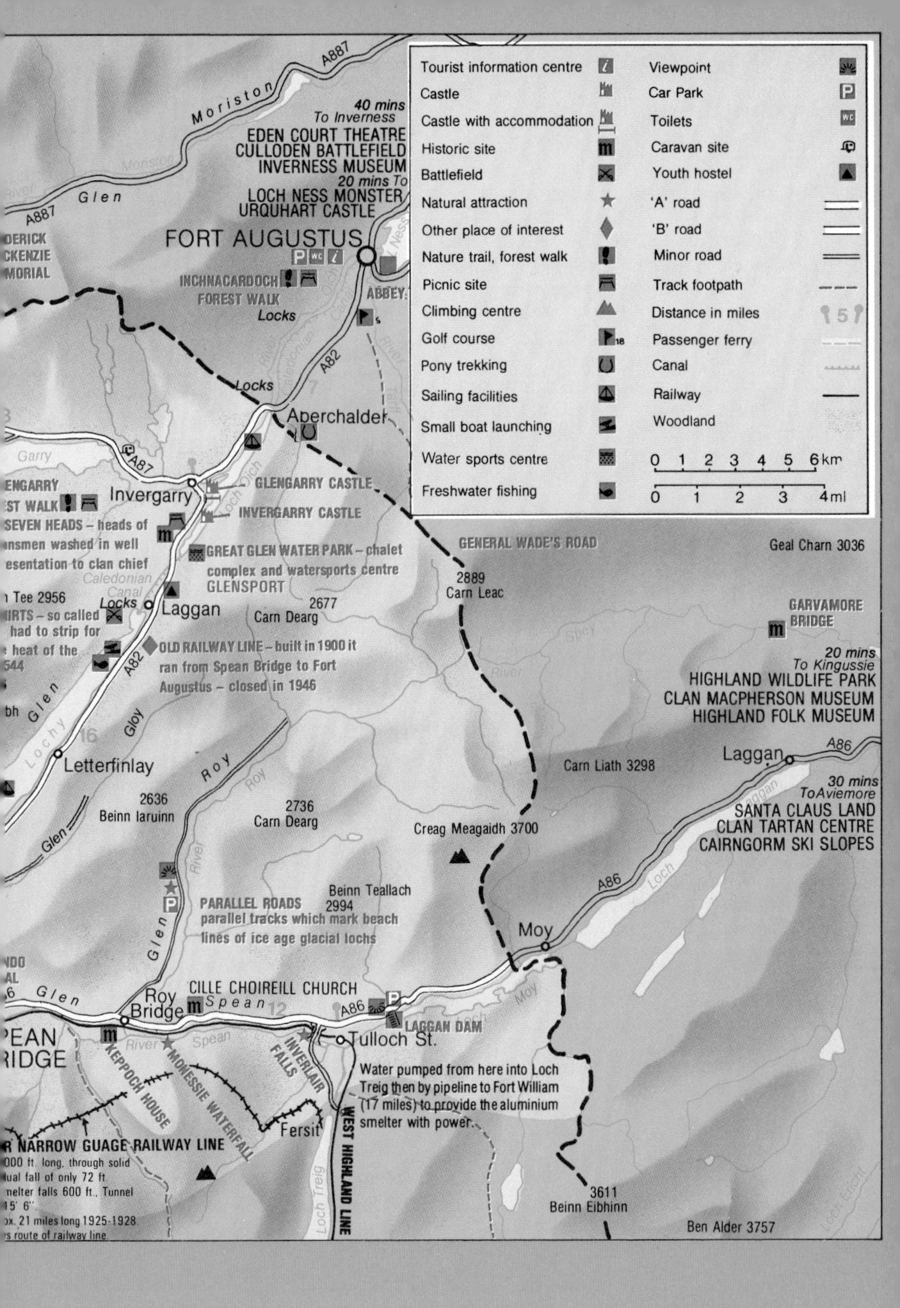

Tourist information centre
Castle
Castle with accommodation
Historic site
Battlefield
Natural attraction
Other place of interest
Nature trail, forest walk
Picnic site
Climbing centre
Golf course
Pony trekking
Sailing facilities
Small boat launching
Water sports centre
Freshwater fishing
Viewpoint
Car Park
Toilets
Caravan site
Youth hostel
'A' road
'B' road
Minor road
Track footpath
Distance in miles
Passenger ferry
Canal
Railway
Woodland
0 1 2 3 4 5 6 km
0 1 2 3 4 ml
A887
Moriston
Glen
40 mins
To Inverness
EDEN COURT THEATRE
CULLODEN BATTLEFIELD
INVERNESS MUSEUM
20 mins To
LOCH NESS MONSTER
URQUHART CASTLE
FORT AUGUSTUS
INCHNACARDOCH
FOREST WALK
ABBEY
Locks
A82
Aberchalder
A87
Garry
Invergarry
GLENGARRY CASTLE
INVERGARRY CASTLE
GREAT GLEN WATER PARK – chalet complex and watersports centre
GLENSPORT
Caledonian Canal
Locks
Laggan
2677
Carn Dearg
OLD RAILWAY LINE – built in 1900 it ran from Spean Bridge to Fort Augustus – closed in 1946
Gloy
Glen
Lochy
Letterfinlay
2636
Beinn Iaruinn
Roy
2736
Carn Dearg
GENERAL WADE'S ROAD
2889
Carn Leac
Geal Charn 3036
GARVAMORE BRIDGE
Spey
River
20 mins
To Kingussie
HIGHLAND WILDLIFE PARK
CLAN MACPHERSON MUSEUM
HIGHLAND FOLK MUSEUM
Laggan
A86
Carn Liath 3298
30 mins
To Aviemore
SANTA CLAUS LAND
CLAN TARTAN CENTRE
CAIRNGORM SKI SLOPES
Creag Meagaidh 3700
Beinn Teallach
2994
PARALLEL ROADS
parallel tracks which mark beach lines of ice age glacial lochs
Moy
Loch
CILLE CHOIREILL CHURCH
Roy Bridge
Spean
A86
LAGGAN DAM
Tulloch St.
Water pumped from here into Loch Treig then by pipeline to Fort William (17 miles) to provide the aluminium smelter with power.
KEPPOCH HOUSE
MONESSIE WATERFALL
INVERLAIR FALLS
Fersit
WEST HIGHLAND LINE
Loch Treig
NARROW GUAGE RAILWAY LINE
3611
Beinn Eibhinn
Ben Alder 3757
Loch Ericht

Spean Bridge

About ten miles north-east of Fort William lies the hamlet of Spean Bridge which derived its name from the bridge over the River Spean built by Telford in 1819. The remains of an older bridge, **Highbridge**, built by General Wade in 1736, can be seen about two miles to the west standing high above the gorge. Access to Highbridge is by way of a track leading off the main road about one mile before reaching Spean Bridge. The bridge itself was quite remarkable as it spanned the precipitous gorge some 100 feet above the tumbling waters below. It was here at Highbridge that the very first skirmishes took place in the 1745 rising. This happened on 16 August 1745 when a body of Government troops, who were making their way from Inverness to reinforce the garrison at Fort William, were ambushed at the bridge crossing by a handful of MacDonell clansmen who, by their tactics, fooled the Government troop commander into believing that the bridge was heavily defended. The Government troops retreated from this bottleneck but were overtaken by the MacDonells, who had been joined by other clansmen led by their chief Keppoch, at the head of Loch Lochy. After a brief engagement the Government troops surrendered and were taken prisoners. This was three days before Prince Charlie actually raised his Standard at Glenfinnan and the prisoners were marched to Glenfinnan to show Prince Charlie the results of the first victory of the Rising.

After crossing the bridge the road forks, one branch going to Inverness and the other eastwards through Glen Spean to Loch Laggan, and we will travel along this eastern branch of the road for the time being. About three-quarters of a mile from the bridge on your left is a substantial dwelling named **Tirnadris House**, standing on a rise. The present house, known locally as Tirindish, replaces an older one which was put to the flame after Culloden, but it was the laird of this house who led the small band of MacDonells who defended Highbridge during that first engagement of the 1745 rising. He subsequently fought loyally for the cause throughout 1745 and 1746, only to meet the same fate as so many others by being hanged for his participation.

Glen Spean near Roy Bridge

Roy Bridge

About three miles from Spean Bridge we cross the River Roy by a new bridge, which was completed in 1966 as a result of a road reconstruction and re-alignment scheme. Until then the normal crossing was by another bridge which was built by Telford in 1817. Just before the bridge there is a little road leading down to **Keppoch House**, which lies on the west bank of the River Roy just before that river tumbles into the River Spean and thereby loses its identity. Keppoch House was the ancestral home of the MacDonells of Keppoch, a branch of the Clan MacDonald. The first house or dwelling-place erected on the site goes back to the beginning of the sixteenth century, when the sixth chief of the clan built his home, or castle (as a chieftain's home was usually called), on a mound right at the junction of the rivers Roy and Spean and which, at that time, was surrounded by a moat. After the 'Keppoch Murders' the castle was pulled down by the MacDonell clansmen stone by stone so that nothing remained to remind them of the horror of the deed perpetrated within the walls of the castle. A second castle was built on the site only to be razed to the ground after Culloden. The present house was built by the seventeenth chief, Ranald, towards the end of the eighteenth century.

To return to the **Keppoch Murders** – this was unquestionably the most infamous event which occurred at Keppoch. Donald Glas, the eleventh chief of the MacDonells of Keppoch, was one of the hardy Highland chiefs who had taken part in that astonishing march of Montrose's from Fort Augustus to Inverlochy and had served under him at that battle. When Donald Glas died he left two sons, Alexander and Ranald, and the elder, Alexander, was still a minor. So at that time the affairs of the clan were placed in the hands of Alisdair Buidhe, one of Alexander's uncles. This arrangement was not to the liking of a branch of the clan known as Sioll Dughaill, who themselves had secret ambitions about the chiefship and were supported in this aim by a small number of other members of the clan. Two years after their father's death Alexander and Ranald returned to Keppoch after completing their education in Rome and Alexander lost no time in arranging a banquet to celebrate his accession to the chiefship. Among the guests were the father and six sons of the Sioll Dughaill family, who picked a prearranged quarrel with the two boys and murdered them (though at the time they proclaimed that it was an accident). The uncle was suspected of complicity in the murder but this was never proved.

One man who was certain that young Alexander and Ranald were murdered, and who cried out for vengence, was the Keppoch bard Iain Lom. He sought help for his mission of revenge from the MacDonell chief, Glengarry, but Glengarry would not move against the Sioll Dughaill family because he was not absolutely certain that the deaths had not been accidental. Iain Lom was not to be deterred in seeking what he believed to be justifiable revenge, because he was convinced that Alexander and Ranald had been murdered. He turned to Sir James MacDonald of Sleat, in the Isle of Skye, who, in the first instance, also refused help. However, the bard persisted, returning to Skye on a number of occasions, and his powers of persuasion finally convinced Sir James, who applied for and obtained a 'State commission of fire and sword' to avenge the murders of the young chief and his brother. In July 1665 he sent a force of fifty men

Loch Laggan

to the mainland, where Iain Lom met them and led them to the house of the murderers at Inverlair. It took little time to break down the barricades set up round the house and the avenging party slew the murderers in their own house – a similar fate to that of their victims two years previously. Iain Lom cut off the heads of the father and his six sons and had their bodies buried at Inverlair Lodge close by. The bard wished to display his gruesome trophies to Glengarry, who had steadfastly refused him aid, so he roped the heads together, slung them over his shoulder and set off for Invergarry. Just before he got there he stopped and washed the heads at a small well by the shore of Loch Oich. From that time the well has been known as 'Tober-nan-Ceann' (Well of the Seven Heads) and in 1812 a monument was erected over the well by Alisdair, Chief of Glengarry, to commemorate this horrific event. After showing the heads to Glengarry, Iain Lom sent them on to Skye to demonstrate to Sir James MacDonald of Sleat that justice had been done. The headless skeletons were dug up from the grave at Inverlair during the nineteenth century, giving full credence to Iain Lom's actions.

Inverlair Lodge has another claim to some distinction in that, after his incredible flight from Germany to Scotland in May 1941, Rudolf Hess, the Deputy Leader of Nazi Germany, was interned there for a time when it was occupied by the Commandos.

A little more than two miles from Roy Bridge you will see a track winding up the hillside, flanked by a number of quite conspicuous cairns. This track leads to the ancient church and burial ground of **Kilchoireil** where many eminent clansmen of Keppoch were laid to rest, including the bard Iain Lom.

Loch Laggan

The dam at the western extremity of Loch Laggan was completed in 1933. This was the second stage of a development to provide power to drive the turbines which provided the electrical power to operate the British Aluminium smelter at Inverlochy. The first stage of the development began in 1924, when work was started on driving a tunnel fifteen feet in diameter through the very heart of the Ben Nevis massif to carry the waters of Loch Treig to Inverlochy. This tunnel is some fifteen miles long. The final stages of the transfer can be seen running into the smelter in the form of five six-foot-diameter pipes over half a mile long and dropping down some 800 feet directly to the power house situated on flat ground at the foot of Ben Nevis just outside Fort William. This first part of the work was completed in 1929. In order to increase the water storage capacity, it was decided to dam Loch Laggan and channel the additional water thus provided to Loch Treig by a fourteen-foot-diameter tunnel some two and three-quarter miles long. As well as raising the level of the loch the dam increased its length from seven to eleven and a half miles. A third stage designed to increase the catchment area was completed in 1943 when the headwaters of the River Spey were diverted to Loch Laggan via another tunnel, this time one of ten foot diameter and some two miles long. All in all a really remarkable piece of engineering.

Glen Roy

If you continue on the road by Loch Laggan it will take you to Aviemore and the Cairngorms, which is well worth a visit but goes beyond the boundaries encompassed by this book, so we will return to Roy Bridge and turn northwards into Glen Roy to see the extraordinary phenomenon of the **'parallel roads'**. When the valley opens out you can see very distinctly these green-swathed roads, three in all, following roughly parallel routes along the mountains on both sides of the valley. In olden times it was believed that the 'roads' were the work of the legendary Fingal, who was credited with making

Glen Roy and the 'parallel roads'

that other natural masterpiece Fingal's Cave on the Isle of Staffa. However, the 'roads', which are gravel ledges about thirty feet wide, were formed by deposits on the shore during the last ice-age, when a massive glacier flowing northwards off Ben Nevis halted the outlets from Glen Roy, Glen Gloy, parallel to Roy, and part of Glen Spean. The lowest of the parallel 'roads' can be seen in all three glens but in none so distinctly as in Glen Roy. The mass of water flowing down from the mountains formed deep lakes and the 'roads' were the shores of these lakes. When the glacial ice was breached or it retreated, the water level sank and new beaches were formed. In Glen Roy the three 'roads', as one would expect from beaches around a lake, are at exactly the same height above sea level all round the glen. The lowest of the three is 857 feet above sea level and the highest 1,149 feet, with the middle 'road' at 1,068 feet. One of the 'roads' is easily reached from the car park up the glen and it is easy to appreciate how they appeared so distinctive. In a sea of heather the surface of the 'roads' is covered only by grass or bracken and they slope gently to what was the water's edge.

While gazing on the wide expanse of the glen and contemplating the remarkable 'roads' it may be recalled that as Glen Roy was a branch glen, with plenty of pure water and many a recess in the hills, it had its fair share of illicit whisky stills in days gone by.

Commando War Memorial

If we return to Spean Bridge and take the Inverness road we come, after a short climb, to the very striking memorial by Scott Sutherland to

Commando War Memorial, near Spean Bridge

those Commandos who fell in the Second World War. It was erected in 1952 and unveiled by Queen Elizabeth, the Queen Mother, in September of that year. It was placed in its elevated position so that it could command a truly panoramic view of Lochaber which, during the war years, was witness to the training of these very special troops, a unique body of highly trained men who went on to win no fewer than thirty-eight battle honours during the war. The Commando Association battle honour flag was laid up in St George's Chapel, Westminster Abbey in 1971 and it enumerates the military operations in which these battle honours were so courageously won.

Mucomir

The road divides at the Commando memorial: one goes north through the Great Glen and the other branches westwards to Gairlochy and this is the one we will follow in the first instance. At Mucomir, just a little under two miles from the monument, the road crosses over a deep man-made gorge. This was cut to provide an outlet for the waters of Loch Lochy when the Caledonian Canal was being built, because the natural outlet was included in the canal system. The water thus diverted poured through this cut and tumbled over the edge into the River Spean in a spectacular waterfall. This man-made waterfall was absorbed into the hydro-electric power scheme when the dam was built in 1962. Just above the dam stands the farmhouse of Mucomir and for many years this was the home of another famous Cameron who gained his reputation in fields other than battlefields. He was Alexander Anthony Cameron, more popularly known just as 'Mucomir'. Without any doubt he was one of the finest heavy athletes that Scotland has ever produced. He died in 1951. It was at Mucomir that the clans gathered under the leadership of Viscount Dundee before the battle of Killiecrankie in 1689.

Gairlochy

About half a mile from the bridge we come to the scattered settlement of Gairlochy on the Caledonian Canal. There are two locks here and the lower one is situated where the River Lochy originally flowed. When the upper lock was constructed in 1844 the water level of the loch was raised twelve feet and it was the resultant surplus water which was fed through the specially cut channel to Mucomir. The lock-keepers' houses here are similar to those at Banavie with their very large bow windows.

Achnacarry

Continuing northwards from Gairlochy the road runs through woodland, parallel to the shore of Loch Lochy but not close to it, and in just two miles on the left of the road there is a private drive leading to **Achnacarry House**, the home of Lochiel, chief of Clan Cameron. This has been the seat of the Cameron chiefs since they moved from Tor Castle towards the end of the seventeenth century. It is this same Achnacarry which is mentioned under Tor Castle, in the Fort William section, where the Camerons and the MacIntoshes were preparing for battle when a mediator in the form of Campbell of Glenorchy intervened and achieved a peaceful settlement. The first castle was built when the clan chief moved from Tor Castle and it was this first edifice which was sacked and burned down by Government troops after Culloden in 1746. As a result of Lochiel's support of Prince Charlie all the clan lands were forfeited and 'gentle Lochiel', as he was known, went into exile with the Prince, never again returning to his homeland. The clan

lands were restored to the Camerons in 1784 and it was Donald, the grandson of the 'gentle Lochiel', who commissioned the building of the present castle which was started in 1802. Unfortunately the bright social life of London was more attractive than Achnacarry to Donald and his wife, and no further work was done to the house, after the walls and roof were in place, until Donald's son, the twenty-third chief, also Donald, had the work completed in 1837. It was this building which was taken over by the Commandos during the Second World War and used as the Commandos Basic Training Centre.

As the Camerons were such fervent and loyal supporters of the Jacobite cause, and indeed his immediate fugitive companions were Camerons, it was natural that Prince Charlie should spend some of that time skulking and hiding in and around the Achnacarry estate when he was a hunted fugitive for five months after Culloden. About one and a half miles further north at Clunes the road turns inland from Loch Lochy and shortly after the road runs through the **'Dark Mile'** made famous by the English novelist D. K. Broster. The Dark Mile was so named because, when the beech trees were in their prime, the branches and leaves interwove above the narrow track and excluded the daylight. Nowadays the track has been widened into a road, some of the beeches have gone and what remains is a very pleasant combination of conifers and deciduous trees, but they do not banish daylight. On the south side of the Dark Mile is the site of Prince Charlie's tree, a hollow one, long since gone, where it is said he took desperate refuge one day when surprised by a patrol of Government troops but, although the site is marked on maps, there is some doubt about the authenticity of the tale. However, on the north side of the Dark Mile Cameron of Clunes lived in a rude hut up on the hillside, when he too was a fugitive after Culloden, and for some time he sheltered the Prince in this primitive abode. Further up the hill and under the bluff of a small cliff is a well-concealed cave which was used as a safe hiding place when the hunt for the Prince was getting close. Caves were often used by the Prince for shelter during his wanderings and some of his treks can almost be traced by the number of Prince Charlie's caves sprinkled over the mainland and the Hebrides.

Loch Arkaig

Loch Arkaig

At the end of the Dark Mile and just before you reach the eastern end of Loch Arkaig a small bridge takes the road over the River Cia-aig. At this point the river cascades into a deep pool which bears the name of the **Witch's Cauldron**. The tale is told that after a prolonged period when the cattle were plagued by some strange sickness, the Camerons who lived here believed that it was caused by someone who was casting their 'evil eye' on them. So they sought advice from an old local seer who told them that they were correct in what they believed, and that the guilty party was an old hag who lived in a hut by the shores of Loch Arkaig. Moreover, the spell would not be lifted until they had rid themselves of the old woman. When the Camerons descended on the old woman they found the hut empty except for a great striped cat who crouched in a corner hissing and spitting at them. The clansmen, dirks at the ready, advanced on this outraged animal but it was too quick for them and beat a hasty retreat through the open door. However, it did not escape without receiving a couple of nasty dagger wounds. These enabled the clansmen to track the beast by a trail of its blood right to the top of the Cia-aig waterfall, where they trapped the stricken animal. As they moved in to finish it off, the great cat let out a fearful screech and leaped over the falls into the pool below, but before it reached those dark waters it changed its form into that of the old woman. The clansmen scrambled down to the side of the pool and finished their mission by stoning the old witch to death while she was still in the pool. Miraculously the cattle slowly recovered from their strange sickness and it never returned.

Just beyond the Witch's Cauldron you reach Loch Arkaig and when you stand by its still waters it seems that time too has stood still; the peace of the loch wraps its mantle around you and it is easy to let your mind be transported to a by-gone era. Then in your mind the peace can be broken by the memory of the intensive hunt for Prince Charlie after Culloden, which was carried out in this area – the shouted orders when the search was in progress – but the mountains do not change and serenity returns. This is a Highland glen which has escaped the imprint of industrial development, though there is some modest tourist incursion which does not detract from the beauty and tranquillity of the place. One of the reasons for the calm character of the place must surely be because there is no through road to the west coast. For the sturdy there are well-marked tracks along the two passes from the head of the loch, Glen Dessary to the north-west and Glen Pean almost due west – but they are not afternoon strolls. It was along the north shore of the loch that Prince Charles rode swiftly immediately after Culloden to shelter for the night in the house of Donald Cameron of Glen Pean, then continued his journey through the glen on foot to Loch Morar and escaped to the Outer Hebrides. After his fugitive wanderings he finished up in the mountains north of Loch Arkaig some five months later. Finally he passed along the south shore of Loch Arkaig on his way to Loch nan Uamh and his escape to France.

Just a little way after you reach the loch you will spy a small island which contains the burial ground of the Macphees of this district and the ruins of a chapel. In recent times this island was one of the few known nesting places of the Osprey. A pair set up a nest at the turn of the century but unfortunately the nests were repeatedly vandalised for their eggs despite reasonable precautions; the ospreys left the nest in 1908 and have not returned since. Now the only place to see ospreys in the nest in Scotland is at Loch Garten in Inverness-shire where they have been successfully nesting and hatching their eggs since 1959.

Towards the head of the loch is the settlement of **Murlaggan** and it was in and around this village that part of a shipment of six casks of French 'louis d'or' was hidden during the period from after Culloden until the Prince finally departed Scotland. This shipment had been landed in the hope of sustaining resistance or even re-kindling the fire of rebellion. Although further resistance was considered by Lochiel and other clan chiefs, firm handling of the situation by Government troops to quell any such movement convinced the chiefs to abandon any such plans. It was then that it was decided to bury the treasure and it was used from time to time over the next few years to finance various Jacobite causes including some large disbursements for the support of some of the exiles' families. Tradition has it that some of the treasure still lies buried near

Murlaggan but the evidence does not support such a belief.

Letterfinlay

If we return to the Commando War Memorial and turn left up the main road to Fort Augustus and Inverness the route takes us up the eastern side of Loch Lochy and in about six miles the route passes through Letterfinlay. Here some forty seriously wounded clansmen, who were fleeing the Cumberland butchery after Culloden, reached the inn and were given shelter by the innkeeper. Most of them had reached the end of their tether and died in the inn. The landlord, fearful of retribution by Government troops for sheltering the clansmen, threw their bodies into Loch Lochy. Some of the bodies were recovered at the north end of the loch and buried there.

Laggan

Some four miles from Letterfinlay and at the head of Loch Lochy we reach Laggan, which is at the entrance to another section of the Caledonian Canal. The two locks at Laggan allow the shipping traffic to enter the highest part of the canal which is 106 feet above sea level.

By the side of the loch, on a level piece of ground, which was eventually submerged when the level of the water in Loch Lochy was raised during the building of the canal, one of the fiercest if not the greatest of all clan battles was fought. The site is called **'Blar nan Leine'**, which translated means 'flat ground of the shirts', and is so called because, on the day of the battle, it was so hot that the clansmen took off their belted plaids, which in those days was a combined kilt and plaid, and fought in their only other garments – their shirts. If the weather was hot the statistics of the engagement are quite chilling. The battle was fought between the Frasers and a combined gathering of Clanranald MacDonalds, Camerons and MacDonells of Glengarry. The strength of the Fraser force was some 300 men but they were outnumbered two to one by their opponents. By the end of this steaming, bloody day there were only

Loch Lochy

Well of the Seven Heads

four Frasers left alive whereas out of the 600 Camerons, MacDonalds and MacDonells there remained alive but eight. It is strange that the battle is recalled more because it was fought in shirts rather than because of the resultant wholesale carnage.

Well of the Seven Heads

At the northern end of this stretch of the Caledonian Canal the road crosses the Laggan Swingbridge and in just over half a mile on the east side of the road is the monument 'Tober-nan-Ceann' or Well of the Seven Heads which was erected to commemorate the grisly events which flowed from the Keppoch Murders, which tale is related under Roy Bridge. The inscription on the monument, which records the reason for its erection, is written in Gaelic, French and Latin as well as English.

Invergarry

At Laggan you cross the borders of Lochaber into the Glengarry MacDonells lands. The route takes you along the western shores of Loch Oich, which unlike Loch Lochy and Loch Ness is a shallow loch and had to be dredged during the construction of the canal. The dredging proved difficult because of the many trunks of large oak trees which in years gone by had been washed down into the loch and were preserved in the peat at the bottom. About one mile north of the Well of the Seven Heads, on the east of the road and overlooking the loch, is the substantial ruin of **Invergarry Castle**, the former home of the clan chiefs, the MacDonells of Glengarry. It was to this castle that the bard Iain Lom came when he unsuccessfully appealed for help in avenging the Keppoch Murders. Prince Charles stayed here after his march from Glenfinnan and was also given shelter during his escape after Culloden. Because of the MacDonells' support of the Jacobite cause, the castle was put to the flame in 1746 and since that time has remained a ruin.

The 'Glen Garry' Highland bonnet was popularised by MacDonell of Glengarry during the royal visit to Edinburgh in 1822.

Fort Augustus

Half a mile past the castle the road divides, going west to Shiel Bridge and the Kyle of Lochalsh and north to Fort Augustus. In about two and a half miles the road comes to the end of Loch Oich and crosses to the east of the canal at Aberchalder where Prince Charles reviewed 2,000 clansmen during his march south in the August of 1745. Four miles further and you will reach Fort Augustus where the canal steps down into Loch Ness by means of five very impressive and quite closely spaced locks. The settlement at Fort Augustus was formerly called Kilchumein and was named Fort Augustus after William

Augustus, Duke of Cumberland, after Wade had rebuilt the fort in 1742. In 1867 the Government sold the fort to Lord Lovat, who presented it to the Catholic Benedictine Order for the foundation of an Abbey and School. The foundation stone was laid that same year but the building was not completed until 1880, gaining Abbey status in 1882.

For those admirers of Robert Burns, the grave of John Anderson lies in the burial ground of the Protestant church. He was made famous by Burns's poem 'John Anderson my Jo John'. He was a carpenter friend of the bard and made Burns's coffin.

Tomdoun and Kinlochhourn

The road west from Invergarry brings you in the space of a few miles to the eastern end of Loch Garry, the site of a fish hatchery, and a few miles beyond this the fairly recent main road turns northwards away from Loch Garry, up into Glen Moriston and then westwards to the Kyle of Lochalsh and the Isle of Skye. But we will proceed westwards along the loch side. This route takes you along the old 'road to the isles' and it was at Tomdoun that the old road struck northwards. Tomdoun is renowned as an angler's retreat and lies at the very heart of some spectacular scenery. The road proceeding westwards from Tomdoun is the only motor road which touches the borders of the remote region of Knoydart. It passes through Glen Garry and along the shores of Loch Quoich before winding its way through the valley of the River Hourn to Kinlochhourn at the head of that most beautiful of sea lochs, Loch Hourn, and here the motor road ends. This is another of these routes which instils in the traveller that sense of 'getting away from it all'.

The Caledonian Canal at Fort Augustus

Part 2, Scottish Miscellany

The Highland Clans

It is my experience that most visitors to the Highlands of Scotland are almost invariably interested in the Highland clans. I find too that those visitors from overseas and from south of the border are often interested in tracing any clan connections when they have known Scottish antecedents. For this reason I am including this short section on the Highland clan system and I have also included a list of the Highland clans and their septs. The map shows what was the general distribution of the clans and the clan lands, but this must be taken as a general guide only and there is no intention to try and define precise boundaries between clans. Nevertheless, it does give a fair representation of the areas of influence and land tenure of the old Highland clans.

The question as to who were the progenitors of the Highlanders of Scotland has never been fully answered and despite the additional evidence that scientific archaeological discovery is throwing up, the question is not likely to be answered to everyone's satisfaction for years to come – if ever. However, a great deal is known about the general picture although the detailed picture is sometimes not quite so clear. Although no chronicles have been discovered to produce documentary evidence to describe the spread of the Celts, the Albans or the Gaels throughout Europe, there is sufficient evidence to acknowledge their influence by present-day names in European geography. No less so was this the case in Britain. However, there is also the theory that, in the very sparsely populated area of the Highlands, the aboriginals remained in the more remote areas and played their part in the creation of the nation – so the scientific debate will go on. The Gael connection can be traced through such names as Galway in Ireland and Galloway in Scotland, while the influence of the Albans is recognised in the ancient name of Scotland, which was Alba, and also in the titles of the Duke of Albany and the Marquis of Breadalbane. As recently as sixty years ago there were reports that in the fastness of some of the more remote hill areas of Albania, from whence the original Albans are believed to have sprung, the population was structured in a tribal system similar to the Scottish clan system where they still wore a type of tartan kilt and where the bagpipes were played by those remote Highlanders. It is fairly well agreed that the Picts came into the country from across the North Sea. When Caesar came to Britain the Celts which he found were probably immigrants from France, and there have remained ever since close ties between French Celts and Scottish Highland, Irish and Isle of Man Celts. But nowhere is the tie so strong as between Scotland and France. From the time that the Romans invaded Britain in AD 43 until they left in AD 410 they were never able to subdue Caledonia, as they called that part of Scotland north of Antonine's Wall (from the Forth to the Clyde). It was this division of Scotland by Antonine's Wall and the influence of the Roman Empire to the south which separates the development of that part of Scotland north of the Forth and Clyde from that part of the Lowlands south of that dividing line. The descendants of the Caledonians were much influenced by the Norsemen during the period from the eighth century to 1266 when they were finally driven from the country. The Caledonian Picts called their land Alba. The sixth century was an important one in the development of Scotland in that the Irish or Dalriadic Scots invaded western Caledonia and established the kingdon of Dalriada. It was also during this century in 563 that St Columba landed on the shores of Iona from Ireland.

So much for the very early times. All these and subsequent events led to the introduction of many new names, even to the use in some cases of surnames during the eleventh century, although surnames were not in general use in the Highlands until the seventeenth century and in some cases later than that. As these invading or immigrant nations were all structured in some feudal form or another they laid the basis of what eventually became a Highland clan system, if system is indeed the appropriate word for it. Few would argue that the Scottish clan system as a social structure has created great interest throughout the world. The word 'clan' or 'children' is the Gaelic equivalent of 'family' and it is this family connotation which separates the Highland clan system from other purely feudal social fabrics. In the 'family' there are no class barriers although there is, of course, a pecking order. But this simple allegiance to the family instilled that brand of loyalty and pride of belonging which was not apparent in other feudal or tribal systems. At the height of the clan system the saying 'proud as a Scot' became common all over Europe. In Scotland the territorial connection played a large part in the adherence to certain clans. Members of clans were not always or necessarily blood relations to the clan chief or his offspring but, nevertheless, when becoming a member of a clan the kinship aspect was the strong element. Being bound to the chief by a bond of kinship rather than serfdom and being part of the larger family gave the clan structure a unique quality. The principle was carried further in that the clan chief bore allegiance to the Chief of Chiefs which eventually evolved into bearing allegiance to the king. At the clan chief's home or castle all members of the clan were always welcome and were treated according to their station in the clan, but the ties between the chief and the clansmen were those of members of the family. This pride of ancestry and family allegiance influenced the Highland clansman's character in that he took pride in the family and in the name of the family was prepared to perform heroic actions, and even the poorest Highlander would suffer great hardship without complaint. Once again it was this element of family that made the difference. It is this same factor of

loyalty of a clan to its chief which has perpetuated the clans in their modern guise as clan societies. Most of these clan societies, which flourish not only in Scotland and the United Kingdom but all over the world, are actively engaged in financing histories, magazines, establishing museums and even acquiring land and property in their respective native clan lands, but probably above all in keeping alive the philosophy of kinship and making welcome these kinfolk from overseas when they visit the 'auld country'. So if you are not already well versed in your family tree perhaps with a glance through the clans and their septs you may even be able to claim membership of one of these clan societies.

Fiery Cross

The military structure and order of battle of the clans was precise and was clearly laid down by clan law and understood by all members of the clan. The obligation of military service was a bounden duty for every able-bodied clansman and when summoned by the Chief there was no denying his call. Every clan had a known and well-established rendezvous or place of assembly. When danger threatened or a sudden emergency arose the clansmen were summoned by the 'crois' or 'Crann-tàra', the fiery cross as it was more commonly known. The cross itself was small, wooden and simply fashioned from two pieces of wood lashed together. One end of the horizontal piece was burnt and usually started its journey still afire or smouldering, while at the other end of the horizontal piece there would be attached a white cloth dipped in blood, usually goat's blood and often from a goat specially killed for the occasion. Then a runner, holding the small cross aloft, would set off on his prearranged route as fast as his legs would carry him and shouting the clan rallying cry as he sped along. He would be the first of a team and he would deliver the cross into the hands of the next member of what was in effect a relay team, who would then, in turn, after completing his part of the route pass it on to another clansman until the whole clan territory had been warned. Depending on the disposition of the clan settlements sometimes two runners were used speeding in opposite directions. It is interesting to note that the fiery cross was still being used in 1745 in relation to Prince Charlie's call to arms. As well as rallying the clan to arms in support of any particular venture it can be used to rally the clans for just the opposite cause. One of the occasions in 1745 when it was used was by Lord Breadalbane, who despatched it throughout the Campbell lands around Loch Tay; it travelled a distance of thirty-two miles in something under three hours. In this case the object of the summons was to assemble his clan and prevent them joining the other clans supporting Prince Charles. However, some thirty years previously, in the 1715 rising, the cross had gone around the same route but then with a different object. On that occasion some 500 clansmen assembled under the chief's banner that very same evening and under the Laird of Glenlyon set off to join the Earl of Mar to take part in the 1715 rising.

One of the last occasions on which the fiery cross was used was during the winter of 1812/13, when the chief of the Highlanders in Glen Garry (Canada) sent the cross around to summon his men in order to repel a raid by the American forces. All in all it was a remarkably efficient method of mobilising a large fighting force in days when any communication had to be carried over ground.

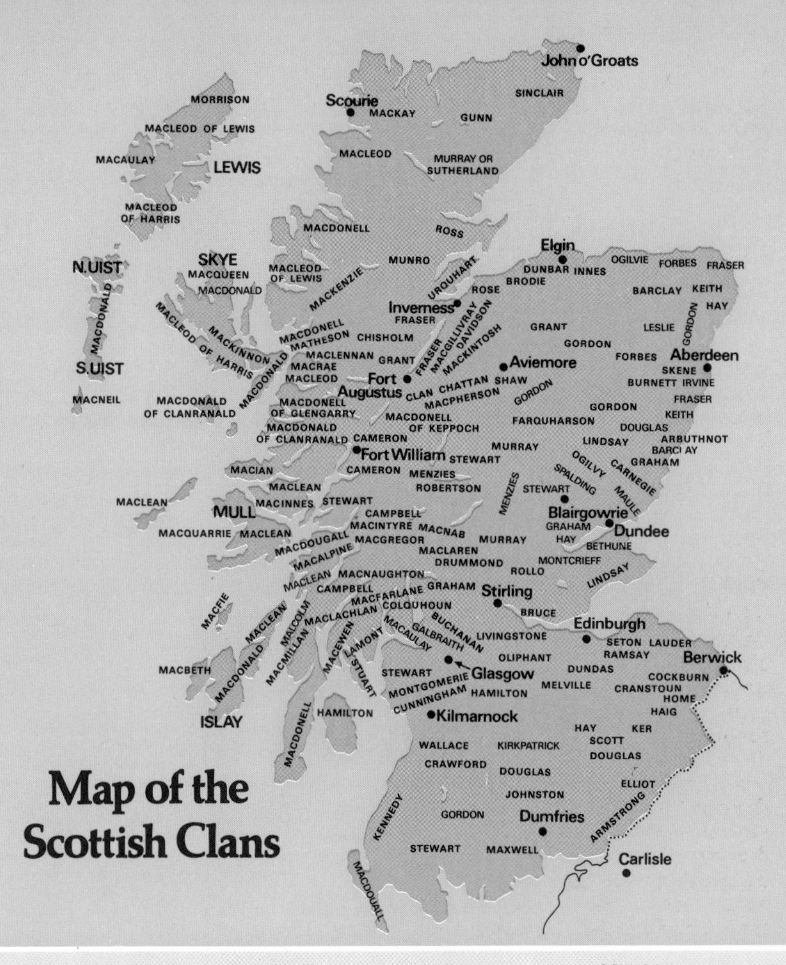

Map of the Scottish Clans

Clans and Their Septs

Clan Buchanan

Colman.
Donleavy.
Donlevy.
Dove.
Dow.
Dowe.
Gibb.
Gibson.
Gilbertson.
Harper.
Harperson.
Lennie.
Lenny.
Macaldonich.
Macandeoir.
MacAslan.
MacAuselan.
MacAuslan.
MacAusland.
MacAuslane.
MacCalman.
MacCalmont.
MacCammond.
MacChruiter.
MacColman.
MacCormack.
Macdonleavy.
MacGibbon.
MacGilbert.
Macgreusich.
Macinally.
Macindeor.
Macindoe.
Mackinlay.
Mackinley.
MacMaster.
MacMaurice.
MacMurchie.
MacMurchy.
Macnuyer.
MacWattie.
MacWhirter.
Masterson.
Murchie.
Murchison.
Risk.
Ruskin.
Spittal.
Spittel.
Watson.
Watt
Yuill.
Yuille.
Yule.

Clan Cameron

Chalmers.
Clark.
Kennedy.
MacChlerich.
MacChlery.
MacGillonie.

Macildowie.
MacKail.
Maclerie.
MacMartin.
MacOnie.
MacOurlic.
MacPhail.
MacSorley.
MacUlric.
Macvail.
MacWalrick.
Martin.
Paul.
Sorley.
Taylor.

Clan Campbell

Bannatyne.
Burns.
Burnes.
Burnett.
Connochie.
Denoon.
Denune.
Harres.
Harris.
Haws.
Hawson.
MacConnechy.
MacConochie.
MacGibbon.
Macglasrich.
MacIsaac.
MacIver.
MacIvor.
MacKellar.
MacKessock.
MacKissock.
MacLaws.
MacLehose.
MacNichol.
MacOran.
MacOwen.
MacPhedran.
MacPhun.
MacTause.
MacTavish.
MacThomas.
MacUre.
Tawesson.
Thomas.
Thomason.
Thompson.
Thomson.
Ure.

Clan Campbell of Breadalbane

MacDiarmid.
MacDermid.

Clan Campbell of Cawdor

Caddell.
Calder.

Clan Campbell of Loudoun

Hastings.
Loudoun.

Clan Chattan

See names under Mackintosh and Macpherson.

Clan Colquhoun

Cowan.
Kilpatrick.
Kirkpatrick.
Macachounich.
MacCowan.

Clan Cumming

Buchan.
Comine.
Comyn.
MacNiven.
Niven.
Russell.

Clan Davidson

Davie.
Davis.
Dawson.
Dow.
Kay.
Macdade.
Macdaid.
MacDavid.

Clan Drummond

Grewar.
Gruer.
Maccrouther.
Macgrewar.
Macgrowther.
Macgruder.
Macgruther.
MacRobbie.

Clan Farquharson

Brebner.
Coutts.
Farquhar.
Findlay.
Findlayson.
Finlay.
Finlayson.
Greusach.
Hardie.
Hardy.
MacCaig.
MacCardney.
MacCuaig.
MacEarachar.
MacFarquhar.
Machardie.
Machardy.
MacKerchar.
MacKerracher.
Mackindlay.
Mackinlay.
Reoch.
Riach.
Tawse.

Clan Ferguson

Fergus.
Ferries.
MacAdie.
MacFergus.
MacKerras.
MacKersey.

Clan Forbes

Bannerman.
Fordyce.
Michie.
Watson.
Watt.

Clan Fraser

Frissell.
Frizell.
Macimmey.
MacGruer.
MacKim.
MacKimmie.
MacShimes.
MacSimon.
MacSymon.
Sim.
Sime.
Simpson.
Simson.
Syme.
Symon.
Tweedie.

Clan Gordon

Adam.
Adie.
Crombie.
Edie.
Huntly.
Milne.
Todd.

Clan Graham

Allardice.
Bontein.
Bontine.
Buntain.
Bunten.
Buntine.
MacGibbon.
MacGilvernock.
Macgrime.
Menteith.
Monteith.

Clan Grant

Gilroy.
MacGilroy.
Macilroy.

Clan Gunn

Gallie.
Gaunson.
Georgeson.
Henderson.
Jameson.
Jamieson.
Johnson.
Kean.
Keene.
MacComas.
MacCorkill.
MacCorkle.
MacIan.
MacKames.
MacKeamish.
MacKean.
MacRob.
MacWilliam.
Manson.
Nelson.
Robison.
Robson.
Sandison.
Swanson.
Williamson.
Wilson.

Clan Innes

Dinnes.
Ennis.
Innie.
McRob.
McTary.
Marnoch.
Mavor.
Middleton.
Mitchell.
Reidfuird.
Thain.
Wilson.

Clan Lamont

Black.
Brown.
Bourdon.
Burdon.
Lamb.
Lambie.
Lammie.
Lamondson.
Landers.
Lemond.
Limond.
Limont.
Lucas.
Luke.
Lyon.
Macalduie.
MacClymont.
MacGilledow.
MacGillegowie.
Macilzegowie.
Macilwhom.
MacLamond.

MacLucas.
MacLymont.
MacPatrick.
MacPhorich.
MacSorley.
Meikleham.
Patrick.
Sorley.
Toward.
Towart.
Turner.
White.

Clan Leslie

Bartholomew.
Lang.
More.

Clan Lindsay

Crawford.
Deuchar.

Clan MacAllister

Alexander.

Clan MacAulay

MacPhedron.
MacPheidiran.

Clan MacArthur

Arthur.
MacCartair.
MacCarter.

Clan MacBean

Bean.
MacBeath.
MacBeth.
Macilvain.
MacVean.

Clan MacDonald

Beath.
Beaton.
Bethune.
Bowie.
Colson.
Connall.
Connell.
Darroch.
Donald.
Donaldson.
Donillson.
Donnelson.
Drain.
Galbraith.
Gilbride.
Gorrie.
Gowan.
Gowrie.
Hawthorn.
Hewison.
Houstoun.
Howison.
Hughson.
Hutcheonson.
Hutcheson.
Hutchinson.
Hutchison.
Isles.
Kellie.
Kelly.
Kinnell.
Mac a'Challies.
MacBeath.
MacBeth.
MacBheath.
MacBride.
MacCaishe.
MacCall.
MacCash.
MacCeallaich.
MacCodrum.
MacColl.
MacConnell.
MacCook.
MacCooish.
MacCrain.
MacCuag.
MacCuish.
MacCuithein.
MacCutcheon.
MacDaniell.
Macdrain.
MacEachern.
MacEachran.
MacElfrish.
MacElheran.
MacGorrie.
MacGorry.
MacGoun.
MacGowan.
MacGown.
MacHugh.
MacHutchen.
MacHutcheon.
MacIan.
Macilreach.
Macilriach.
Macilleriach.
Macilrevie.
Macilvride.
Macilwraith.
MacKean.
MacKellachie.
MacKellaig.
MacKelloch.
MacKiggan.
MacKinnell.
MacLairish.
MacLardie.
MacLardy.
MacLarty.
MacLaverty.
MacLeverty.
MacMurchie.
MacMurdo.
MacMurdoch.
MacO'Shannaig.
MacQuistan.
MacQuisten.
MacRaith.
MacRorie.
MacRory.
MacRuer.
MacRurie.
MacRury.
MacShannachan.
MacSorley.
MacSporran.
MacSwan.
MacWhannell.
Martin.
May.
Murchie.
Murchison.
Murdoch.
Murdoson.
O'Drain.
O'May.
O'Shannachan.
O'Shaig.
O'Shannaig.
Purcell.
Revie.
Reoch.
Riach.
Rorison.
Shannon.
Sorley.
Sporran.
Train.
Whannel.

Clan MacDonald of Clanranald

Allan.
Allanson.
Currie.
MacAllan.
MacBurie.
MacEachin.
MacGeachie.
MacGeachin.
MacIsaac.
MacKeachan.
Mackechnie.
MacKeochan.
MacKessock.
MacKichan.
MacKissock.
MacMurrich.
MacVarish.
MacVurrich.
MacVurie.

Clan MacDonald of Ardnamurchan

Johnson.
Kean.
Keene.

Clan MacDonald of Glencoe

Henderson.
Johnson.
Kean.
Keene.
MacHenry.
MacIan.
MacKean.

Clan MacDonell of Glengarry

Alexander.
Sanderson.

Clan MacDonell of Keppoch

MacGillivantic.
MacGilp.
Macglasrich.
MacKillop.
MacPhilip.
Philipson.
Ronald.
Ronaldson.

Clan MacDougall

Carmichael.
Conacher.
Cowan.
Dougall.
Livingston.
Livingstone.
MacConacher.
MacCowan.
MacCoul.
MacCulloch.
MacDulothe.
MacHowell.
MacKichan.
MacLucas.
MacLugash.
MacLulich.
MacNamell.
Macoul.
Macowl.

Clan MacDuff

Abernethy.
Duff.
Fife.
Fyfe.
Spence.
Spens.
Wemyss.

Clan MacFarlane

Allan.
Allanson.
Bartholomew.
Caw.
Galbraith.
Griesck.
Gruamach.
Kinnieson.
Lennox.
MacAindra.
MacAllan.
MacCaa.

MacCause.
MacCaw.
MacCondy.
MacEoin.
MacGaw.
MacGeoch.
Macgreusich.
Macinstalker.
Maclock.
MacJames.
Mackinlay.
MacNair.
MacNeur.
MacNider.
MacNiter.
MacRob.
MacRobb.
MacWalter.
MacWilliam.
Miller.
Monach.
Napier.
Parlane.
Robb.
Stalker.
Thomason.
Weaver.
Weir.

Clan Macfie

Duffie.
Duffy.
MacGuffie.
Machaffie.

Clan MacGillivray

Gilroy.
MacGillivour.
MacGilroy.
MacGilvra.
MacGilvray.
Macilroy.
Macilvrae.

Clan MacGregor

Black.
Caird.
Comrie.
Dochart.
Fletcher.
Gregor.
Gregorson.
Gregory.
Greig.
Grewar.
Grier.
Grierson.
Grigor.
Gruer.
King.
Leckie.
Lecky.
MacAdam.
Macara.
Macaree.
MacChoiter.
MacConachie.
Maccrouther.
Macgrewar.
Macgrowther.
Macgruder.
Macgruther.
Macilduy.
MacLeister.
MacLiver.
MacNee.
MacNeish.
MacNie.
MacNish.
MacPeter.
MacPetrie.
Malloch.
Neish.
Nish.
Peter.
White.
Whyte.

Clan Macinnes

Angus.
MacAngus.
MacCainsh.
MacCansh.
MacMaster.

Clan Macintyre

Tyre.
MacTear.
Wright.

Clan Mackay

Bain.
Bayne.
MacCay.
MacCrie.
Mackee.
Mackie.
MacPhail.
Macquey.
Macquoid.
Macvail.
Neilson.
Paul.
Polson.
Williamson.

Clan MacKenzie

Kenneth.
Kennethson.
MacBeolain.
MacConnach.
MacIver.
MacIvor.
MacKerlich.
MacMurchie.
MacMurchy.
MacVanish.
MacVinish.
Murchie.
Murchison.

Clan Mackinnon

Love.
Mackinney.
Mackinning.
Mackinven.
MacMorran.

Clan Mackintosh

Adamson.
Ayson.
Clark.[1]
Clarke.[1]
Clarkson.[1]
Clerk.[1]
Combie.
Crerar.
Dallas.
Doles.
Elder.
Esson.
Glen.
Glennie.
Hardie.
Hardy.
MacAndrew.
MacAy.
MacCardney.
MacChlerich.[1]
MacChlery.[1]
MacCombie.
MacCombe.
MacComie.
M'Conchy.
MacFall.[1]
Macglashan.
Machardie.
Machardy.
MacHay.
Mackeggie.
M'Killican.
Maclerie.[1]
MacNiven.[1]
MacOmie.
MacPhail.[1]
Macritchie.
MacThomas.
Macvail.[1]
Niven.
Noble.
Paul.
Ritchie.
Shaw.
Tarrill.
Tosh.
Toshach.

Clan MacLachlan

Ewan.
Ewen.
Ewing.
Gilchrist.
Lachlan.
Lauchlan.
MacEwan.
MacEwen.
MacGilchrist.

Clan Maclaine of Lochbuie

MacCormick.
MacFadyen.
MacFadzean.
MacGilvra.
Macilvora.
MacPhadden.

Clan MacLaurin

MacFater.
MacFeat.
MacPatrick.
MacPhater.
MacGrory.
MacRory.
Paterson.

Clan Maclean

Beath.
Beaton.
Black.
Clanachan.
Garvie.
Lean.
MacBeath.
MacBheath.
MacBeth.
Macilduy.
MacLergain.
MacRankin.
MacVeagh.
MacVey.
Rankin.

Clan Maclennan

Lobban.
Logan.

Clan MacLeod of Harris

Beaton.
Beton.
MacCaig.
MacClure.
MacCrimmon.
MacCuaig.
MacHarold.
Macraild.
Norman.

Clan MacLeod of Lewis

Callum.
Lewis.
MacAskill.
MacAulay.
MacCaskill.
MacLewis.
MacNicol.
Tolmie.

Clan Macmillan

Baxter.
Bell.
Brown.
MacBaxter.

Clan Macnab

Abbot.
Abbotson.
Dewar.
Gilfillan.
Macandeoir.

Clan MacNaughton

Hendre.
Hendry.
Kendrick.
MacBrayne.
Maceol.
MacHendrie.
MacHendry.
MacKendrick.
MacKenrick.
Macknight.
MacNair.
MacNayer.
MacNiven.
MacNuir.
MacNuyer.
MacVicar.
Niven.
Weir.

Clan MacNeil

MacNeilage.
MacNeiledge.
MacNelly.
Neal.
Neil.
Neill.

Clan Macpherson

Cattanach.[1]
Clark.[1]
Clarke.[1]
Clarkson.[1]
Clerk.[1]
Currie.
Fersen.
Gillespie.
Gillies.
Gow.
Lees.
MacChlerich.[1]
MacChlery.[1]
MacCurrach.[1]
MacGowan.
Maclerie.[1]
MacLeish.
MacLise.
MacMurdo.
MacMurdoch.
MacMurrich.
MacVurrich.
Murdoch.
Murdoson.

Clan Macquarrie

MacCorrie.
MacCorry.
MacGorrie.
MacGorry.
MacGuaran.
MacGuire.
Macquaire.
Macquihrr.
Macquire.
MacWhirr.
Wharrie.

Clan Macqueen

MacCunn.
MacSwan.
MacSwen.
MacSween.
MacSwyde.
Swan.

Clan Macrae

Macara.
MacCraw.
Macra.
Macrach.
MacRaith.
MacRath.
Rae.

Clan Malcolm

MacCallum.
Malcolmson.

Mar Tribe

Marr.
Morren.
Strachan.
Tough.

Clan Mathieson

MacMath.
MacPhun.
Mathie.

Clan Menzies

Dewar.
Macindeor.
MacMenzies.
MacMinn.
MacMonies.
Means.
Mein.
Meine.
Mennie.
Meyners.
Minn.
Minnus.
Monzie.

Clan Munro

Dingwall.
Foulis.
MacCulloch.
MacLulich.
Vass.
Wass.

Clan Morison

Brieve.
Gilmore.
MacBrieve.

Clan Murray

MacMurray.
Moray.
Rattray.
Small.
Spalding.

Clan Ogilvy

Airlie.
Gilchrist.
MacGilchrist.
Milne.

Clan Robertson

Collier.
Colyear.
Donachie.
Duncan.
Duncanson.
Dunnachie.
Inches.
MacConachie.
MacConnechy.
MacDonachie.
Macinroy.
MacIver.
MacIvor.
Maclagan.
MacRobbie.
MacRobie.
MacRobert.
Reid.
Roy.
Stark.
Tonnochy.

Clan Ross

Anderson.
Andrew.
Dingwall.
Gillanders.
MacAndrew.
MacCulloch.
MacLulich.
MacTaggart.
MacTear.
MacTier.
MacTire.
Taggart.
Vass.
Wass.

Clan Sinclair

Caird.
Clouston.
Clyne.
Linklater.
Mason.

Clan Skene

Cariston.
Dis.
Dyce.
Hallyard.
Norie.

Clan Stewart

Boyd.
Garrow.
Menteith.
Monteith.
Carmichael.
MacMichael.

Stewart, Appin

Carmichael.
Combich.
Livingston.
Livingstone.
MacCombich.
Mackinlay.
Maclae.
Maclay.
Maclea.
Macleay.
MacMichael.

Stewart, Atholl

Crookshanks.
Cruickshank.
Duilach.
Gray.
Macglashan.

Stuart, Bute

Bannatyne.
Fullarton.
Fullerton.
Jameson.
Jamieson.
MacCamie.
MacCloy.
MacCaw.
MacKirdy.
MacLewis.
MacMunn.
Munn.
MacMutrie.

Clan Sutherland

Cheyne.
Federith.
Gray.
Keith.
Mowat.
Oliphant.

[1] *These are directly of Clan Chattan, and not of Mackintosh or Macpherson*

Some Gaelic Roots

Aber — *mouth or confluence of a river*
Aird, ard — *height, promontory*
Allt, ault — *stream*
An — *of the*
Aros — *dwelling*
Auch, ach — *field*

Bal, baile — *town, homestead*
Ban — *white, fair*
Beag, beg — *little*
Bealach, balloch — *mountain pass*
Ben, beann, beinn — *mountain*
Bhuidhe, bui, vuie — *yellow*
Brae, braigh, bread — *upper part*
Breac, vrackie — *speckled, variegated*

Cam, cambus — *crooked*
Carn, cairn — *heap of stones*
Ceann, ken, kin — *head, end*
Cil, kil — *church*
Clach, cloich — *stone*
Clachan — *place of stones, helmet*
Cnoc — *hill, knoll*
Coille, killie — *wood*
Coire, corrie — *hollow*
Creag, craig — *rock, cliff*
Cruach — *rick, stack*
Cul, coul — *back, recess*

Darach — *an oak*
Dearg — *red*
Druim, drum — *ridge, back*
Dubh, dhu — *black, dark*
Dun — *hill fort*

Eaglais — *church*
Eas, esh — *waterfall, ravine*
Eilean — *island*

Fada — *long*
Fail — *rock, cliff*
Fionn, fyne — *white, shining*

Garbh, garve — *rough, rugged*
Gearr, gair — *short*
Geo, gia, gio — *chasm, rift*

Holm — *uninhabited island*
How, haugr — *burial mound*

Inch, innis — *island*
Inver, inbhir — *mouth of a river*

Kil — *church, burying-place*
Knock — *knoll*
Kyle — *a strait, a firth*

Lag, laggan — *hollow*
Larach — *site of an old ruin*
Larig — *pass, mountain track*
Learg — *pass, hill-slope*
Liath — *grey*
Linn, linne — *pool*
Loch — *lake*
Lochan — *small lake*

Machar — *plain by the sea*
Maol, meal, mam — *bald headland*
Mor, more — *great, extensive*
Moy — *a plain*

Na, nam, nan — *of the*

Ochter — *high-lying*

Poll — *pool*

Quoich, cuach — *cup*

Reidh — *smooth*
Ru, rhu, row, rudha — *point*

Sgor, scuir, sgurr — *sharp rock*
Strath — *broad valley*
Strone, sron — *nose, promontory*
Struan, sruth — *stream*

Tarbert, tarbet — *isthmus*
Tigh, tay — *house*
Tobar — *well*
Torr — *round hill, heap*

Uamh — *cave 'weem'*
Uig — *nook, sheltered bay*
Uisge, esk — *water*

Voe — *narrow bay*

Gifts and Souvenirs – *What to buy*

Very few people who visit a country or indeed a holiday resort in their own country can resist the very natural desire to purchase some memento of their visit and I am sure people visiting Lochaber will be no different. The choice of such a souvenir or gift to take home is and always will be a personal one which will necessarily meet the criteria of the person purchasing it. However, sometimes the range is bewildering and it might be useful to set down some of those gifts you can purchase in Scotland which are indeed native to the country. You will always be able to get many and varied gifts of the 'heather and tartan' variety and this indeed may be all that you require to recall your visit to Scotland, and if you seek diligently there are some very attractive souvenirs in this category. If, however, you wish to widen your horizons and look for something different then perhaps the following ideas might stimulate your own thoughts when making a choice.

Scottish spun and manufactured tartan, tweed and woollen goods are readily available and these are always very popular. Other types of memento may include polished stones, etchings on slate, gem stones set in traditional ancient Scottish mountings, grouse claws in a silver setting, objects carved from a stag's horn, perhaps a carved walking stick or silver jewellery from the Orkney and Shetland Islands. Then perhaps you might be interested in a modern craftsman-made targe, dirk or skean dhu. In recent years there has been a great revival of local pottery manufacture and there are a number of local potteries spread throughout the district. This is one area where personal choice is paramount. In my experience some of these are excellent but others fall short of excellence and you must judge them on their merits when you visit them. In this land of bens and glens the magnificent scenery cries out to be painted and there are many pictures on offer in local shops at quite modest prices. Then there is glassware. One of the most successful and imaginative projects of recent years was the establishment of Caithness Glass Ltd in Wick in 1960. It set out to produce high-quality, hand-blown glassware of chaste design. Continental craftsmen were engaged initially to train the local youth and in a matter of some ten years or so 90 per cent of the glassware produced by Caithness Glass was accepted by the Council of Industrial Design for the Design Index. The quality of Caithness glass now bears an international reputation. If you are interested in seeing the whole process from the mixing of the raw materials to the final glass-blowing stage then perhaps you will be able to organise a visit to the branch of the works in Oban. So there are a few ideas to stimulate thoughts on the question of souvenirs and gifts.

Polished stones from Scotland

Evening Entertainment

Nobody in his or her right mind would argue that entertainment in the evening was the great magnet that pulled the visitor to Lochaber. However, everybody who does come to stay in Lochaber necessarily has to spend evenings there as well as the days. So, when you have drunk to the fill from the scenic goblet and switched off the image of the historical past you may well ask the question, 'What does the region offer in the way of entertainment in the evening?' Throughout the area you will always find hotels or pubs which organise some form of entertainment in the evening, and many of them do this on a regular basis with local singers, musicians and dancers taking part. You will almost certainly be able to take part in that traditional form of entertainment the 'Ceilidh', pronounced '*Kay*-li'. For the uninitiated, a Ceilidh is a cross between a concert, a variety show and a party and is the very essence of hospitable Scottish entertainment. It is an informal get-together for the sheer enjoyment of music, dancing, singing, poetry, storytelling and any other entertainment talents. It is an occasion when everybody unselfconsciously gets involved or should do. It really is a grand way of spending an evening. Another popular entertainment in many hotel bars and pubs is folk-music by local folk groups and in this instance when I say local, I mean Scottish in that one often finds itinerant Scottish folk groups from other parts of Scotland. I certainly have many pleasant memories of this type of entertainment and what stands out in my memory on several occasions was the sheer virtuosity of the fiddlers and the players of the various types of 'squeeze-box'. Oh yes, the time between each day of exploration can be very happily filled indeed.

If you seek more formal entertainment I have mentioned in Part 3 the Eden Court Theatre (Telephone (0463) 221718). If you are staying overnight in Inverness, this theatre offers a quite remarkable range of productions. Also just within range if one intends to stay overnight or perhaps take in a matinee on a Wednesday or Saturday, is the Pitlochry Festival Theatre (Telephone (0796) 2680 – 75 miles away and Scotland's 'theatre in the hills'). It was a remarkable act of faith when this theatre was set up in a marquee over thirty years ago and has operated continuously throughout the season from April to October ever since. Now it has a superb brand-new purpose-built auditorium and the scope and range of the productions is again quite remarkable.

Then, of course, you may just require a good meal with a relaxing drink to accompany it and there are many restaurants and hotels which will supply this need. So all in all there is every prospect that you may well enjoy the evenings in their own way just as you enjoy the daylight excursions.

Regional Food – *and the crofting influence*

Elsewhere in Part 3 of this book I have mentioned the 'stockpot' sign which denotes those catering establishments which offer traditional Scottish recipes using home-grown Scottish produce. What is the background to the development of native culinary skills in the Highlands of Scotland? As in many other facets of the development of a country the social structure in Scotland was a dominant factor. In the Highlands this was based on the crofting system which was prevalent throughout the Highlands and still survives to this day though in a much more limited way because of the effect of the Highland clearances. The dour reality of crofting was that it was eternally a fight to make ends meet and in many cases after the 'clearances' this fight became even more difficult as the crofters were moved to less productive plots of land. For this reason, you will always find nowadays that crofters have other occupations as there would be no likelihood of them making a tiny croft an economic viability. Crofting is a system of tenure of cultivated land where the tenant or crofter pays a rent to the owner who at one time was the clan chief or his tacksman. Before the Crofters Act of 1886 – less than 100 years ago – a crofter could be literally thrown off his croft without any notice whatsoever. Since the introduction of the Act, crofting has managed to survive because the tenure is now protected and the crofter also has the right to a fair rent fixed by the Scottish Land Court. However, it is recognised that the small crofter could never become economically viable. In the eighteenth century a crofting family would raise cattle, sheep, goats and poultry. The problem of grazing was solved by the crofting community having common rights to the grazing that existed. The cattle, goats and the sheep produced milk which was converted into cheese and butter. The sheep also produced wool which was used for spinning and weaving and the rearing of cattle remained the only outside source of income.

A typical Highland croft

Sometimes, this was bartered for oatmeal but most of the cattle were driven south to markets along the old droving roads. It was this way of life which dictated the development of the types of food which they ate. In those days the breed of sheep reared was one of small stature and they were very tame, which in turn meant that it was an easy operation to milk them. They also produced mutton of a very fine flavour. The goat population in those early days was very large and used mainly for milking and for their hides. It is on record that in one year towards the end of the seventeenth century no less than 100,000 goat hides were sent to London from the Highlands. Every crofter kept hens for the staple diet of eggs and occasionally poultry. It seems strange that pigs did not figure in the development of stock breeding as it seems a most suitable animal under these conditions. The Highlander has always been acknowledged as a superstitious being and pigs were considered a bad omen. So if you are offered a fine pork chop cooked as 'crofters used to cook it' you can, I am sure, conjure up a suitable retort. You must remember too that few crofts had chimneys, the main fuel was peat and the cooking container was usually a pot suspended over a peat fire. Peat produced a moderate steady heat which was ideal for simmering as well as being ideal for use with the girdle for baking thin oat cakes or the thicker bannocks. Later, the open peat fire was superseded by a cast-iron cooking range but still fired by peat producing the same qualities for cooking. During the eighteenth century visitors to the Highlands have recorded that a great deal of milk from sheep, goats and cows was consumed by the Highlanders as well as copious amounts of buttermilk and whey. So crofter-originated food is likely to be based on boiling and stewing rather than grilling and roasting. The crops grown were potatoes, turnips, leeks, carrots and the only green vegetable used in those early days was young nettles. If the land was good enough, oats and barley were grown. To supplement the diet there was always the harvest from the sea and to the crofter this meant mainly herring and mackerel. Both these fish should be eaten soon after they are caught. Kippers are a comparatively new product compared with salted herring which was a regular winter diet of the crofter in that there was usually a barrel of salt herring in the house to help sustain him throughout the winter months. Shell-fish are common to the west coast though they were despised by the crofter because, to them, they were a sign of desperate poverty and hunger. It is of interest to note that the Pacific oyster is now being farmed in Scotland as well as salmon and trout.

But now we must consider the laird whose diet developed along an entirely different plane from that of the crofter. Here we encompass the game from grouse moors, deer from the forests and salmon from the rivers. Here too we should include the world-renowned Scottish beef in its various forms and cuts. The dairy products of the Highlands consisted mainly of butter and soft cheeses. There were no hard cheeses made in the Highlands – these were developed in southern Scotland. We must include crowdie. This was the name given to what was at one time the staple item of diet of most of the population and it consisted of oatmeal and water. It is sometimes referred to as gruel or brose; as a child I can recall many a day started off with a bowl of oatmeal brose. Nowadays crowdie or Highland crowdie is the name given to a low-fat cheese and there are many crowdie de-

Venison is traditional Scottish fare

rivatives. So there is a wide range of Scottish fare to sample, from those of very humble origin to those worthy of presentation at dinner in the laird's mansion or castle.

From the humbler origins come such delights as Scotch broth and other soups, simply prepared mackerel and herring – I can think of few tastier dishes than the large fresh west-coast herring, caught in the summer months when its fat content is at its greatest, gutted and boned, coated in fine oatmeal and fried to perfection so that it is crisp and golden brown on the outside and soft and succulent on the inside. Then there is a variety of 'stovies' which simply means food produced by that almost standard method of cooking, which was to put the article on the stove and cook it slowly. Stovies will usually include potatoes which are then often layered with other things such as sausages, onions, chicken and limpets. Other shell-fish such as mussels, whelks and cockles are common and are traditionally boiled and eaten with salt, pepper and essentially vinegar.

Moving up the social scale in the development of Scottish food but not necessarily in the taste-bud league, you can have salmon, smoked or perhaps grilled as steaks, and then a choice of game birds from grouse, pheasant, partridge, capercaillie and ducks. However, you must remember that the game birds are only in season from about August to January each year. If venison is your aim then the more common red deer stag season is from July to October and the hind season from October to February.

I hope this short discourse has given you some general indication as to what to expect when you are seeking to sample truly Scottish fare.

Highland Whisky

To the uninitiated, the irreverent, the ignorant or the insensitive, whisky is whisky whether it be made in Scotland, Ireland, Canada, America, Japan or Timbuktoo. But to those who respect, admire and enjoy Highland whisky there is a world of difference between whisky and whiskey and Highland whisky. A famous clansman of mine and a connoisseur of whisky, the late Neil Gunn, said that 'until a man has the luck to chance on a perfectly matured malt, he does not really know what whisky is.'

These few notes are designed merely to enlighten in some small measure the uninitiated and will not in any way form the basis of a guide to Highland whisky. If you wish more guidance on this subject then there are a number of excellent publications which I am sure will absorb your interest for a considerable time.

There are three types of whisky – malt, grain and blended. Malt is made entirely from malted barley. Grain whisky is made mainly from maize (American corn) but can also be made from rye and oats. Blended whisky, which is the type most widely known, is a blend of both malt and grain whiskies.

Malt whisky is usually Highland whisky but may also be of Lowland origins. The necessary ingredients are those items which were and still are so readily obtainable in the Highlands: barley, water and peat. Water is added to the barley, which allows it to germinate. It is then dried in a kiln over a peat fire or furnace to produce the malt. During this drying process the peat smoke is allowed to come up through the barley and it is this which gives it its distinctive flavour. The malt is then ground and mashed with hot water to produce 'wort'. This in turn is cooled, yeast added and fermented in huge vats to produce a liquid known as 'the wash'. It is this 'wash' which is doubly distilled in the huge, characteristic onion-shaped pot stills, the vapour being cooled by passing it through a copper pipe which in turn is passed through cooling water and it is this consequent distillation which is true malt whisky.

In 1830 a new type of still was developed by a gentleman named Coffey, where the alcohol was driven off by steam, and this patent still was able to produce a 95 per cent alcohol spirit out of any type of grain in a continuous process which was cheaper than the pot still process and was not bound by geographical locality. Arguments raged for many years as to whether or not this new spirit should be accorded the title of whisky and it took a Royal Commission in 1909 to finally give it equal status with the traditional Highland whisky. The spirit produced by the patent still was without the body or flavour of malt and was very much sharper to the taste and was closer to a neutral spirit than malt whisky.

It was discovered that subtle blending of malt whisky and grain spirit produced a palatable result. This is blended whisky as we know it today and it is this type of whisky which forms the bulk of all whisky sold at the present time. The blend is usually about 40 per cent malt to 60 per cent grain but this varies. Over recent years there has been a welcome trend for Highland distilleries to increase the marketing of their malt whisky but it will always remain that the bulk of Highland malt whisky is destined to be used in the production of blended whisky. There is no doubt that the blending operation requires great skill and it is this skill which produces the many excellent blended whiskies that are with us today.

Bird Watching in Lochaber

Few would disagree that the great appeal to the visitor to Scotland is its immense variety and quality of scenery and its vivid historical interest. However, Scotland is also a paradise for those visitors who seek their own special interest such as golfing, fishing and sailing. Birdwatching is another interest which falls into this category. Because of its vast areas of unspoilt countryside, Scotland provides a great variety of habitats for birds and the remarkable number of resident and migrant birds in this comparatively small area has always attracted ornithologists from the United Kingdom and indeed from all over the world. There are roughly 160 breeding species in Scotland and such birds as the Scottish Crossbill, Greenshank, Dotterel, Capercaillie, Ptarmigan and the Crested Tit are some of the species which breed virtually nowhere else in the United Kingdom but the Highlands. There are also a number of species of duck, sea birds and divers which are unique to Scotland or at least much more common in the Highlands than anywhere else. Then there is the famous Osprey whose re-establishment in Scotland as a breeding species provides an absorbing story. The majestic Golden Eagle can be seen in many parts of the Highlands and Islands but the exact location of eyries is seldom revealed to strangers by those who know their location and who jealously guard such information. This short section can only give the visitor an indication to what one can reasonably expect to see in the Highlands and around the coasts. For the avid birdwatcher further information should be sought from The Scottish Centre for Ornithology and Bird Protection, 17 and 21 Regent Terrace, Edinburgh, EH7 5BS (Telephone 031–556 6042).

In Morvern the Ardtornish Estate Office compiled a check-list of birds seen in Morvern in 1978 and this gives a good indication as to what one can expect to see in this area. In all, during that year there were positive recorded sightings of 132 species. The sightings included the following:

Divers. These included the winter visitor, the Great Northern Diver, who remains well into spring, and the Black-throated and Red-throated Divers.

Sea Birds. These included the Petrels including Leach's Petrel, the Manx Sheerwater, Fulmars, Gannets, Cormorants, Shags, Razorbills and Guillemots including the black Guillemot.

Geese, Duck and Swans. The wild geese are normally winter visitors but the resident breeding ducks include the Eider, Goosander and the Red-breasted Merganser. The swans seen included the Mute and Whooper.

Below: *Greenshank;* bottom: *Black-throated Diver*

Top: *Golden Eagle;* above: *Eider Ducks*

Birds of Prey. Among those seen were the Golden Eagle, Buzzards, Kestrels, Peregrine Falcons, Merlins, Hen-harriers, Sparrowhawks and Ospreys in passage. Of the owls seen were the Barn Owl, Tawny Owl and the Short-eared Owl.

Waders. Of the waders seen were the Oystercatcher, the Snipe, the Ringed Plover, the Golden Plover and the lovely Greenshank. Also spotted were the Common Sandpiper, the Whimbrel and the Woodcock.

Gulls and Terns. The five common species of Gull were seen as well as Kittiwakes and several varieties of Terns. Both the Great and Arctic Skua were also seen.

Game Birds. Both the red and black Grouse were spotted as well as the Ptarmigan. One of the other birds to look for is the spectacular Capercaillie.

Passerine Birds. There are many of these birds in Scotland and perhaps some of the more interesting ones to mention which were seen were the Great Spotted Woodpecker, the Dipper, the Raven and the Hoodie, various Tits, the Twite, the Red-headed Bunting, the Coal Tit, Tree Creeper, the Ring Ouzel, Wheatear, the Whinchat, Stonechat, Redstart, four types of Warbler, Goldcrest, the Grey Wagtail and the Redpoll.

So this short section should illustrate that the birdwatcher is going to derive a great deal of satisfaction in pursuing his or her hobby in this area.

Below: *Red Grouse;* bottom: *Razorbills*

Part 3, Useful Tourist Information

When you refer to this section of the book with the object of planning something specific to do I would urge you to make full use of the 'What's On' leaflet which is continually up-dated and freely available at the Tourist Information Offices.

General Information

Travel

Bookings for rail, sea and air travel to Scotland and within Scotland should be made through your travel agent, or directly to British Rail, airlines and ferry companies. The Scottish Tourist Board, or the local tourist organisation, in this case the Fort William and Lochaber Tourist Organisation, will be glad to give you information but cannot make your travel bookings for you.

Seats may be booked in advance on the main long-distance coaches and aircraft, and so may berths and cabins in the steamers to the islands. Sleeping berths on trains should always be booked well in advance. It is necessary to book seats for 'extended' coach tours and also for day coach outings operated from most holiday and touring centres.

Car hire and sailing cruiser bookings should also be made in advance wherever possible, especially for July and August.

Accommodation

Any visitor to Scotland who intends to tour widely is well advised to consult the excellent publications issued by the Scottish Tourist Board covering hotels and guest houses, bed and breakfast establishments, self-catering accommodation and camping and caravan sites. However, if you intend to stay over in Lochaber for a shorter or longer spell, which we hope you will, then you are advised to obtain from the Tourist Information Office, Cameron Square, Fort William, Inverness-shire, any of the following free of charge:

(a) *The Best of the Highlands* full colour brochure (Hotel, Guest House and Self-Catering Packages);

(b) Register 1 – Hotel, Guest House and Bed and Breakfast Establishments;

(c) Register 2 – Self-Catering, Caravan and Camping Sites, Activity Holiday Establishments.

Advanced Booking of Holiday Accommodation

Many intending visitors find difficulty in booking their holiday accommodation, and spend money and time writing and telephoning to numerous hotels and guest houses. In an effort to help in this connection the Fort William and Lochaber Tourist Organisation is prepared to undertake the booking for you. Full details of the scheme and an application form are contained in the Registers of Accommodation.

Book a Bed Ahead

If you have not made advance reservations for your accommodation I would strongly advise you to make use of the Scottish Tourist Board's 'Book a Bed Ahead' scheme, which operates throughout Scotland, and is available at all the Tourist Information Centres where the 'bed' symbol is displayed. – ' 🛏 '

You can book your accommodation ahead for the coming night and subsequent nights at any of these Centres, even if your destination is many miles away. It is a guaranteed booking. Hotels, guest houses and bed and breakfast places may all be reserved by means of the scheme.

On making a reservation, the visitor pays a deposit, which is deducted from his bill at the end of his stay. In addition, there is a standard charge for communication (telephone or telex) and for service.

By using this scheme, the holidaymaker may save hours which would otherwise have been spent in trying to find accommodation – and the motorist can also save petrol – and knows exactly where he is going and that a welcome awaits him.

Local Booking Scheme

For those of you who arrive at your destination without having previously booked your accommodation, I would advise you to make use of the Scottish Tourist Board's 'Free Local Booking' scheme, which also operates throughout Scotland and is available at all the Tourist Information Centres where the 'bed' symbol is displayed. – ' 🛏 '

It is a guaranteed booking. Hotels, guest houses and bed and breakfast places may all be reserved by means of the scheme. On making a reservation, the visitor will pay a small deposit which will be deducted from his bill at the end of his stay. Again a welcome will await him.

The Association of Scotland's Self-Caterers

You'll spot this symbol beside many self-catering holidays. The Association was formed to promote higher standards of self-catering accommodation.

Realistic minimum standards have been established – properties vary from simple to luxurious and all are inspected by the Association for accuracy of brochures, cleanliness, comfort, equipment and heating. All in all, you know you have the basis of an excellent holiday.

Further information on member establishments can be obtained from The Association of Scottish Self-Caterers, Mr I. Matheson, Na Tighean Beaga, East Park, Roy Bridge, Inverness-shire. Tel: (039 781) 370 or 436

Driving

The 'Rules of the Road' are the same in Scotland as in the rest of the U.K. While there is limited motorway mileage in Scotland, the roads are uniformly good. In the remoter areas there is a considerable mileage of single-track roads, with frequent passing-places. Please, *never* use these passing-places as laybys – or for overnight parking of caravans. Slow-moving traffic (and motorists towing caravans), are asked to pull in to passing-places, where appropriate, to let faster traffic through.

When touring in this region of Scotland, remember that in some of the more remote areas petrol stations are comparatively few, and distances between them may be considerable. Some petrol stations close on Sundays. Fill your tank in good time, and keep it as full as possible.

Public Holidays

The Bank Holidays which are also general holidays in England do not apply in Scotland. Most Bank Holidays apply to banks and to some

**Most of the general information contained in pages 105–6 is reproduced by the kind permission of the Scottish Tourist Board from their publication* Scotland: Where to Stay, Hotels and Guest Houses.

professional and commercial offices only, although Christmas Day and New Year's Day are usually taken as holidays by everyone. In place of the general holidays, Scottish cities and towns normally have a Spring Holiday and an Autumn Holiday. The dates of these holidays vary but they are almost invariably on a Monday.

Money

Currency, coinage and postal rates in Scotland are the same as in the rest of the U.K. Scotland differs from England in that Scottish banks issue their own notes. These are acceptable in England, at face value, as are Bank of England notes in Scotland. Main banks are open during the following hours:
Monday, Tuesday, Wednesday: 09.30–12.30, 13.30–15.30
Thursday: 09.30–12.30, 13.30–15.30, 16.30–18.00
Friday: 09.30–15.30.
Some city centre banks are open daily 09.30–15.30.

In rural areas, banks post their hours clearly outside and travelling banks call regularly.

Eating

Lunch in restaurants and hotels outside the main centres is usually served between 12.30 and 14.00. Dinner usually starts at 19.00 or 19.30 and may not be served much after 21.00. Where you know you may arrive late it is advisable to make arrangements for a meal in advance. An alternative to dinner is High Tea, usually served between 16.30 and 18.30. See the list of restaurants on pages 108–112.

A Taste of Scotland

When eating out, do not forget to sample a 'Taste of Scotland'. Look out for the 'Stockpot' sign at hotels and restaurants. – ' ❦ ' This indicates that the establishment offers traditional Scottish recipes using the best of Scottish produce. Scottish soups with intriguing names like Powsowdie or Cullen Skink, Aberdeen Angus steaks or venison or game in season; salmon or trout from Scottish rivers, or herring or haddock cured in a variety of ways – and a choice of some thirty varieties of Scottish cheese – these are some of the 'Tastes of Scotland' which add to the enjoyment of a holiday.

Traditional hare soup

Restaurants

Prices are often much reduced at lunchtime when set lunches are available. All meals are subject to 15% VAT (value added tax). This is sometimes included in the prices indicated on the menu and sometimes added to the final bill. A cover charge per person is also sometimes added. This should be stated on the menu. Some restaurants automatically add a service charge, in which case no tipping is necessary. If no charge is included there is in fact no obligation to tip, but most people leave 10% to 15%, depending on the standard of service.

GLENCOE AND LOCH LEVEN

Kings House Hotel. *½ mile off A82, 15 miles south of Glencoe. March to October. Tel: Kingshouse (08556) 259.* Good home cooking and traditional Scottish fare.

Carnoch Restaurant. *A82, 2 miles south of Glencoe. Easter to September. Tel: Ballachulish (08552) 248.* Small, friendly atmosphere, not licensed.

Clachaig Inn. *Old Glencoe Road off A82, 1½ miles south of Glencoe. January to December. Tel: Ballachulish (08552) 252.* Good straightforward meals.

Glencoe Hotel. *In Glencoe village, A82. January to December. Tel: Ballachulish (08552) 245.* Traditional dishes.

The Milk Bar Griddle. *On A82, 1 mile south of Ballachulish Bridge. April to September. Tel: Ballachulish (08552) 369.* All day table service or take-away, not licensed.

Ballachulish Hotel. *Adjacent to bridge. January to December. Tel: Ballachulish (08552) 239.* Good food served in Lochside restaurant or lounge bar.

The Holly Tree. *On A828, 3 miles south of Ballachulish Bridge. January to December, restricted winter. Tel: Duror (063174) 292.* Lochside setting, excellent range of dishes.

Ardsheal House. *2 miles off A828, 3½ miles south of Ballachulish Bridge. April to October. Tel: Duror (063174) 254.* Outstanding for food, wine, service and comfort.

Duror Hotel. *A828, 4½ miles south of Ballachulish Bridge. January to December. Tel: Duror (063174) 219.* Kitchens open 8 a.m.–11 p.m. every day of the year.

Stewart Hotel. *A828, 5 miles south of Ballachulish Bridge. April to October. Tel: Duror (063174) 268.* Cordon Bleu cook, Highland atmosphere.

Loch Leven Hotel. *A82, north side of Ballachulish Bridge. January to December. Tel: Onich (08553) 236.* Traditional and continental dishes.

Creag Dhu Hotel. *A82, 2 miles north of Ballachulish Bridge. April to October. Tel: Onich (08553) 238.* Fine Highland table (with health foods too). Lochside setting.

Allt-Nan-Rhos Hotel. *A82, 2½ miles north of Ballachulish Bridge. April to October. Tel: Onich (08553) 210.* Lochside setting, good home cooking.

Onich Hotel. *A82, 3½ miles north of Ballachulish Bridge. April to October. Tel: Onich (08553) 214.* Lochside setting and gardens, comprehensive range of meals and snacks served all day.

Nether Lochaber Hotel. *A82, by Corran–Ardgour ferry. January to December. Tel: Onich (08553) 235.* Home cooking, good wine list.

SOUTH OF GLENCOE AND LOCH LEVEN

Airds Hotel, Port Appin. *2 miles off A828, 15 miles south of Ballachulish Bridge. April to October. Tel: Appin (063173) 236.* AA Rosette for Dinner, and other symbols of merit.

NORTH ARGYLL

Ardgour Hotel. *West end of Corran–Ardgour ferry. January to December. Tel: Ardgour (08555) 225.* By Corran Narrows. Good home cooking.

Strontian Hotel. *A861, 15 miles west of Corran ferry. January to December. Tel: Strontian (0967) 2029.* By Loch Sunart. Good home cooking.

Loch Sunart Hotel, *Strontian. A861, 15 miles west of Corran ferry. April to October. Tel: Strontian (0967) 2471.* By Loch Sunart, good home cooking.

Strontian Centre. *A861, 15½ miles west of Corran ferry. April to October. Tel: Strontian (0967) 2268.* Self-service restaurant.

Kilcamb Lodge, *Strontian. A861, 16 miles west of Corran ferry. January to December. Tel: Strontian (0967) 2257.* By Loch Sunart. Traditional fare a speciality.

Ben View Hotel. *½ mile off A861, 1½ miles west of Strontian. January to December. Tel: Strontian (0967) 2333.*

Lochaline Hotel. *A884, 33 miles south of Corran ferry. January to December. Tel: Morvern (096784) 226.* Local seafood and game.

Salen Hotel. *A828, 10 miles west of Strontian. January to December. Tel: Salen (096785) 661.* Good straightforward meals.

Clan Morrison Hotel, *Glenborrodale. B8007, 6½ miles west of Salen. April to October. Tel: Glenborrodale (09724) 212.* Lochside setting. AA Rosette for Cuisine.

Glenborrodale Castle. *B8007, 7 miles west of Salen. April to October. Tel: Glenborrodale (09724) 266.* Elegant décor, excellent menu, local seafood and game.

Kilchoan Hotel. *B8007, 19 miles west of Salen. January to December. Tel: Kilchoan (09723) 200.* Good plain food.

Sonnachan Hotel, *Kilchoan. B8007, 3 miles west of Kilchoan. April to October. Tel: Kilchoan (09723) 211.* Most westerly hotel in Britain, traditional food.

Loch Shiel Hotel, *Acharacle. B861, 17 miles south of Lochailort. January to December. Tel: Salen (096785) 224.* Good straightforward meals, steaks, grills and salmon.

THE ROAD TO THE ISLES

Glenfinnan House Hotel. *½ mile off A830, 14 miles west of Fort William. April to October. Tel: Kinlocheil (039 783) 235.* Family-run mansion house, idyllic setting by Loch Shiel.

Stage House Inn, *Glenfinnan. A830, 14 miles west of Fort William. January to December. Tel: Kinlocheil (039 783) 246.* Superb cuisine including local produce.

Lochailort Inn. *A830, 24 miles west of Fort William. January to December. Tel: Lochailort (06877) 208.* Good home cooking, seafood, salmon and venison a speciality.

Glenshian Lodge Hotel, *Lochailort. ½ mile off A861, ½ mile south of Lochailort. April to October. Tel: Lochailort (06877) 235.*

Roshven Farm. *A861, 4 miles south of Lochailort. April to December. Tel: Lochailort (06877) 221.* Good Highland hospitality in restaurant.

Glenuig Inn. *A861, 8 miles south of Lochailort. January to December. Tel: Lochailort (06877) 219.* Cheerful atmosphere, good home cooking. By Glenuig Bay. Local shellfish.

Arisaig House, *Beasdale. A830, 8 miles west of Lochailort. March to October. Tel: Arisaig (06875) 622.* Elegant country house restaurant, limited choice, outstanding quality.

Jacques Place, *Arisaig. A830, 10 miles west of Lochailort. April to October. Tel: Arisaig (06875) 254.* Friendly, small restaurant.

The Old Library, *Arisaig. A830, 10 miles west of Lochailort. April to October. Tel: Arisaig (06875) 651.* Exceptional little restaurant.

Arisaig Hotel. *A830, 10 miles west of Lochailort. April to October. Tel: Arisaig (06875) 210.* Family run establishment, good range of dishes.

Cnoc na Faire Hotel. *A830, 3 miles north of Arisaig. January to December. Tel: Arisaig (06875) 249.* Good home cooking.

Morar Hotel. *A830, 6 miles north of Arisaig. April to October. Tel: Mallaig (0687) 2346.* Mallaig kippers, fresh fish, salmon and venison in season.

Heatherlea Hotel, *Mallaig. ½ mile off A830, 1 mile south of Mallaig. January to December. Tel: Mallaig (0687) 2184.* Friendly, casual atmosphere, seafood dishes.

West Highland Hotel, *Mallaig. A830, 9 miles north of Arisaig. April to October. Tel: Mallaig (0687) 2210.* Specialising in local fresh fish, salmon and venison in season.

Jocobite, *Mallaig. A830, 9 miles north of Arisaig. April to October. Tel: Mallaig (0687) 2133.* Coffee shop and restaurant, relaxed atmosphere.

Marine Hotel, *Main Street, Mallaig. January to December. Tel: Mallaig (0687) 2217.* Family run establishment, good range of dishes. Fresh fish a speciality.

Fisherman's Mission, *Main Street, Mallaig. January to December. Tel: Mallaig (0687) 2086.* Simple home cooking at reasonable prices. (Lunches only.)

FORT WILLIAM AND BEN NEVIS

Croit Anna Hotel. *A82, 3 miles south of Fort William. January to December. Tel: Fort William (0397) 2268/9.* Outstanding for food, wine, service and comfort.

Ladbroke Mercury Hotel. *A82, 2½ miles south of Fort William. January to December. Tel: Fort William (0397) 3117.* High standard, à la carte. Featuring the Lochaber table.

Cruachan Hotel. *A82, ½ mile south of Fort William. January to December. Tel: Fort William (0397) 2022.* Comfortable, pleasant atmosphere.

West End Hotel, *High Street, Fort William. January to December. Tel: Fort William (0397) 2614.* Tasteful décor, good food, bar lunches served daily.

Highland Star, *155 High Street, Fort William. January to December. Tel: Fort William (0397) 3905.* Chinese restaurant, fully licensed, take-away meals available.

Grand Hotel, *High Street, Fort William. January to December. Tel: Fort William (0397) 2928.* Good straightforward meals.

Highland Hotel, *Union Road, Fort William. January to December. Tel: Fort William (0397) 2291.* Homely atmosphere, traditional fare.

McTavish's Kitchen, *High Street, Fort William. (Scottish night and self-service restaurant.) May to September. Tel: Fort William (0397) 2406.* Traditional Highland fare, Scottish entertainment.

Munro Lounge, *103 High Street, Fort William. (Above Ben Nevis Bar.) Tel: Fort William (0397) 2295.* Comfortable, friendly atmosphere, well-priced quality dishes.

Stag's Head Hotel, *High Street, Fort William. April to October. Tel: Fort William (0397) 4144.* Straightforward meals. Reasonable prices.

Angus Restaurant, *66 High Street, Fort William. January to December. Tel: Fort William (0397) 2654.* Popular with varied menu.

Tourist Restaurant, *37 High Street, Fort William. April to October. Tel: Fort William (0397) 2075.* Plain restaurant, but interesting menu, friendly service and good value.

Imperial Hotel, *Fraser Square, Fort William. January to December. Tel: Fort William (0397) 2040.* Good traditional fare.

McTavish's Coffee Shop, *Tweeddale, Fort William. April to October. Tel: Fort William (0397) 2406.* Friendly self-service restaurant.

Nevisport Restaurant, *Airds Crossing, Fort William. January to December. Tel: Fort William (0397) 4921.* Popular eating place, very reasonably priced quality dishes, with Scottish flavour.

Alexandra Hotel, *Parade, Fort William. January to December. Tel: Fort William (0397) 2241.* Traditional fare in friendly atmosphere.

Nevisbank Hotel, *Belford Road, Fort William. January to December. Tel: Fort William (0397) 2595.* Popular, family run, good food.

Nevisbridge Restaurant, *Fort William. A82, 1 mile north of Town Centre. February to December. Tel: Fort William (0397) 4244.* Popular eating place; the food is good too.

Glen Nevis Restaurant, *Fort William. 2½ miles up Glen Nevis. February to November. Tel: Fort William (0397) 5459.* Popular eating place, reasonably priced quality dishes.

Milton Hotel, *North Road, Fort William. 1½ miles north of Town Centre. April to September. Tel: Fort William (0397) 2331.* Modern décor, tasty wholesome food.

Road to the Isles Griddle, *Lochybridge, Fort William. 2½ miles north of Town Centre. April to October. Tel: Fort William (0397) 3152.* Speedily and freshly cooked meals.

Moorings Hotel, *Banavie. A830, 4 miles west of Fort William. January to December. Tel: Corpach (03977) 550.* Extensive menu of well-prepared dishes. Taste of Scotland.

Glen Loy Lodge, *by Banavie. B8005, 3 miles north of Banavie. January to December. Tel: Gairlochy (039 782) 200.* Excellent food and wine in comfortable friendly atmosphere.

Corpach Hotel. *A830, 4½ miles west of Fort William. January to December. Tel: Corpach (03977) 223.* Straightforward meals. All home cooking.

Inverlochy Castle. *A82, 3 miles north of Fort William. April to November. Tel: Fort William (0397) 2177/8.* Luxurious atmosphere, excellent food. (Booking essential.)

Red grouse, roasted to perfection

GLEN SPEAN AND THE GREAT GLEN

Spean Bridge Hotel. *A82, 8 miles north of Fort William. March to December. Tel: Spean Bridge (039 781) 250.* Comfortable, with tasteful décor. Traditional Scottish fare.

Woollen Mill Restaurant, *Spean Bridge. A82, 8 miles north of Fort William. April to October. Tel: Spean Bridge (039 781) 260.* Friendly café.

Bridge Grill, *Spean Bridge. A82, 9 miles north of Fort William. January to December. Tel: Spean Bridge (039 781) 366.* Good basic food.

Roy Bridge Hotel, *Roy Bridge. A86, 5 miles east of Spean Bridge. Open all year. Tel: Spean Bridge (039 781) 236.* Excellent meals in comfortable dining room.

Stronlossit Hotel, *Roy Bridge. A86, 5 miles east of Spean Bridge. January to December. Tel: Spean Bridge (039 781) 253.* Good basic home cooking. Scottish fare.

Kinchellie Croft Motel, *Roy Bridge. A86, 5½ miles east of Spean Bridge. February to October. Tel: Spean Bridge (039 781) 265.* Family run, fresh, home-cooked food.

Glenspean Lodge Hotel, *Roy Bridge. A86, 6½ miles east of Spean Bridge. January to December. Tel: Spean Bridge (039 781) 224.* Comfortable, high standard of cuisine.

Letterfinlay Lodge Hotel, *by Spean Bridge. A82, 8 miles north of Spean Bridge. March to October. Tel: Invergloy (039 784) 222.* Elevated position over Loch Lochy. Good Highland fare. Family run.

Corriegour Lodge Hotel. *A82, 11 miles north of Spean Bridge. January to December. Tel: Invergloy (039 784) 285.* Straightforward meals.

Glengarry Castle Hotel. *A82, 1 mile south of Invergarry. April to October. Tel: Invergarry (080 93) 254.* Quiet and intimate. Good range of dishes.

The Inn on the Garry, *Invergarry. Junction A82/A87. April to October. Tel: Invergarry (080 93) 206.* Traditional Highland table with a chance to sample real Scottish fare.

Tomdoun Hotel, *Tomdoun. 5 miles along Kinlochourn Road off A87, 10 miles west of Invergarry. March to October. Tel: Tomdoun (080 92) 218.* Family run, good Highland fare, friendly atmosphere.

Licensing Laws

Currently in Scotland, the hours that public houses and hotel bars are open to serve drinks are the same all over the country. 'Pubs' are open from 11.00 to 14.30 and from 17.00 to about 23.00, Monday to Saturday inclusive and some are now licensed to open on Sundays. In addition, some establishments may have obtained all-day licences.

Hotel bars have the same hours as 'pubs' and are open on Sundays from 12.30 to 14.30 and 18.30 to 23.00. Residents in licensed hotels may have drinks served at any time. Some restaurants and hotels have extended licences allowing them to serve drinks with meals until 01.00 in the morning.

Churches

The established Church of Scotland is Presbyterian, but the Roman Catholic and other denominations have very considerable numbers of adherents. The Episcopal Church of Scotland is in full communion with the Church of England, and uses a similar form of worship. In the far north and west of Scotland, particularly in the islands, many people belong to the Free Church of Scotland, and these people appreciate it when their views on the Sabbath as a day when there should be no recreational or other unnecessary activity, are respected by visitors. Times of services of the various denominations are usually intimated on hotel notice boards, as well as outside the churches and, of course, visitors are always welcome.

Coming from Overseas

Visitors to Scotland from overseas are required to observe the same regulations as for other parts of the U.K. As a general rule they must have a valid passport and, in certain cases, visas issued by British Consular authorities overseas; check with a local travel agent, or where appropriate, the overseas offices of the British Tourist Authority.

Currency: Overseas visitors who require information about the import and export of currency, cars or other goods, on personal purchases and belongings, shopping concessions, etc., should consult a travel agent or bank or the overseas offices of the B.T.A.

Driving: Motorists coming from overseas who are members of a motoring organisation in their own country may obtain from them full details of the regulations for importing cars, motor cycles, etc., for holiday and touring purposes into the U.K. They can drive in Britain on a current Driving Licence from their own country, or with an International Driving Permit, for a maximum period of twelve months. Otherwise, a British Driving Licence must be obtained: until the Driving Test is passed it is essential to be accompanied by a driver with a British licence.

Seat Belts: Drivers and front seat passengers *must* wear safety belts while driving in Britain.

VAT: Value Added Tax, currently charged at 15% on many goods, can sometimes be reclaimed by overseas visitors who buy items for export. Visitors should ask the shopkeeper about the retail export schemes before making a purchase, and will be required to fill in special forms.

Rabies

Britain is *very* concerned to prevent the spread of rabies. Strict quarantine regulations apply to animals brought into Britain from abroad and severe penalties are enforced if they are broken or ignored. Dogs and cats are subject to six months quarantine in an approved quarantine centre. Full details from the Department of Agriculture and Fisheries for Scotland, Chesser House, 500 Gorgie Road, Edinburgh, EH11 3AW. The restrictions do not apply to animals from Eire, Northern Ireland, the Isle of Man or the Channel Islands.

Tourist Information Offices

(in or near the region)

Fort William ☛ Fort William and Lochaber Tourist Organisation. *Tel: Fort William (0397) 3581 (General enquiries), 3781 (24 hr Ansaphone)*
January–December

Aviemore ☛ Spey Valley Tourist Organisation. *Tel: Aviemore (0479) 810363*
Telex: 75127
January–December

Ballachulish ☛ Tourist Information and Interpretative Centre. *Tel: Ballachulish (085 52) 296*
May–September

Broadford, Isle of Skye ☛
Tourist Information Centre. *Tel: Broadford (047 12) 361/463*
Easter–mid-September

Fort Augustus 🛏 Information Centre, Car Park, Fort Augustus. *Tel: Fort Augustus (0320) 6367.*
Mid-May–mid-September

Glencoe Visitor Centre (NTS). *Tel: Ballachulish (085 52) 307*
April–October

Glenfinnan Monument (NTS) by Fort William. *Tel: Kinlocheil (039 783) 250*
1 April–mid-October

Inverness 🛏 Inverness, Loch Ness and Nairn Tourist Organisation, 23 Church Street. *Tel: Inverness (0463) 34353*
Telex: 75114
January–December

Kyle of Lochalsh 🛏 Information Centre. *Tel: Kyle (0599) 4276*
Easter–September

Mallaig 🛏 Information Centre. *Tel: Mallaig (0687) 2170*
May–September

Oban 🛏 Oban, Mull and District. *Tel: Oban (0631) 3122 or 3551*
January–December

Portree, Isle of Skye Tourist Information Centre. *Tel: Portree (0478) 2137*
Telex: 75202
January–December

Edinburgh 🛏 Scottish Tourist Board, 5 Waverley Bridge, Edinburgh, EH1 1BQ. *Tel: 031–226 6591, 031–225 8821*

Glasgow 🛏 Information Bureau, George Square, Glasgow, G2 1ES. *Tel: 041–221 7371/2, 041–221 6136/7*
Telex: 779504

London Scottish Tourist Board, 5/6 Pall Mall East, London. *Tel: 01–930 8661/2/3*

Useful/Emergency Telephone Nos.

Doctor: *Fort William 3136, 2017, 3773 or 2947 for appointment.*
Dentist: *Fort William 2147 or 2501 for appointment.*
Chemists: *Macfarlane & Son, High Street, Fort William. Tel: 2031. Boots Ltd, 19 High Street, Fort William. Tel: 2038*
Hospital: *Belford Hospital, Fort William. Tel: 2481.*
Police & Mountain Rescue Stations: *Fort William 2361/2, Arisaig 222, Glencoe 222, Mallaig 2171/2, Spean Bridge 2222, Strontian 2022.*
Post Offices/Bureau de Change: Head Office: *Fort William 2122.*
Banks/Bureaux de Change:
Bank of Scotland:
Arisaig. Tel: Arisaig 272. 62 High Street, Fort William (Keycard). Tel: Fort William 3497. Mallaig. Tel: Mallaig 2370.
Clydesdale Bank:
58 High Street, Fort William (Autobank). Tel: Fort William 3590.
Royal Bank of Scotland:
Ballachulish (sub-office). Tel: Ballachulish 368. Corpach, by Fort William. Tel: Corpach 531. 6 High Street, Fort William (Cashline). Tel: Fort William 2010 or 2208. Leven Road, Kinlochleven. Tel: Kinlochleven 212. Mallaig. Tel: Mallaig 2232.
Trustee Savings Bank:
6 Tweeddale, High Street, Fort William. Tel: 2029.

Transport Facilities

Rail:

London (Euston) to Fort William. There is an overnight direct 'sleeper' service London (Euston) to Fort William. Sundays to Fridays (*not* Saturdays).
Glasgow (Queen Street) to Fort William. There are daily services to

Fort William from Glasgow. Mondays to Saturdays (*not* Sundays). Journey time: approximately 4½ hrs.

Fort William to Mallaig. This railway was mentioned in the introduction to the Fort William section.

On Mondays to Saturdays during the summer months a Saloon Car is conveyed on the 12.55 train from Fort William to Mallaig and the 16.10 from Mallaig to Fort William.

A supplement (£1 in 1982) is payable for each single journey and, as accommodation is limited, it is recommended that you make advance reservations at the Fort William or Mallaig ticket offices.

An historic and scenic commentary will normally be provided.

Bus and Coach: Long Distance

A long-distance coach service is run from Fort William to Glasgow, Edinburgh, Inverness, Oban and Portree by *Highland Omnibuses Ltd. Tel: Fort William (0397) 2373* or *Head Office, Inverness (0463) 37575*. A service to Glasgow is run on weekdays (*not* Sundays) from May to September by *Skyways Travel. Tel: Kyle 4328*.

Glasgow (Buchanan Bus Station) to Fort William. Twice daily service. Journey time: approximately 3 hrs 20 mins. This bus continues through to Uig, Skye to connect with the Outer Isles ferry service.

Edinburgh (Bus Station) to Fort William. On Saturdays only, in the summer. Journey time: 4 hrs 45 mins.

Fort William to Inverness. Thrice daily service on weekdays and once on Sundays. Journey time: 2 hrs 20 mins.

Fort William to Oban. Thrice daily service on weekdays (*not* Sundays). Journey time: approximately 2 hrs.

Fort William to Portree. Service on weekdays (*not* Sundays). Journey time: 3 hrs 30 mins.

Bus and Coach: Local Services

Fort William to Glen Nevis. On weekdays there is a five times daily service to Glen Nevis from the Bus Station in Fort William and twice on Sundays. Journey time: 15 mins. Mid-May to mid-September.

Fort William. There are frequent daily services to Inverlochy, Caol, Banavie and Corpach.

Mallaig, Morar, Arisaig. A local service in this area is run by Morar Motors, Morar. *Tel: Mallaig 2118*.

Ferries

Current timetables are available in the Tourist Information Offices.

Corran to Ardgour. There is a continuous service 8 a.m. to dusk or 8 p.m. whichever is the earlier, for vehicles and passengers, across these narrow waters. January to December.

Kyle of Lochalsh to Kyleakin (Skye). Frequent service for vehicle and passengers. Weekdays and Sundays. January to December.

Glenelg to Kylerhea (Skye). Frequent car and passenger service daily on weekdays (*not* Sundays). Summer only.

Mallaig to Armadale (Skye). May to September: Five times daily service Mondays to Saturdays for cars and passengers. October to April: restricted passenger service only on certain days.

Lochaline to Fishnish (Mull). Service for both cars and passengers. Sailing time: 15 mins. There are also connections to Tobermory and Oban. January to December.

The Lochaline ferry

Fort William to Camusnagaul. Passenger only service. January to December.

Mingary Pier (Kilchoan) to Tobermory (Mull). Passenger only service throughout the summer.

The Small Isles. There are passenger ferries operating in the summer months:

1. Mallaig to Eigg, Muck and Rhum. (Limited winter service.)
2. Arisaig to Eigg and Muck.
3. Glenuig to Eigg.

Oban to Iona. There is a twice daily service from Oban to Craignure (Mull) thence by synchronised coach service across Mull to Fionnphort and then by ferry (10 mins.) to Iona.

Oban to Craignure (Mull) There is a regular car ferry and passenger service operating daily throughout the year.

Helicopter

(Burnthills Aviation Ltd. Tel: Fort William 4182 for reservations). There are twice daily services between Fort William, Oban, Lochgilphead, Rothesay and Glasgow.

Coach Tours

There are some very fine coach tours available from Fort William, Onich and Ballachulish for those who have come to Lochaber without a car or those who wish to unburden themselves for a while from the stress of driving which we all, apparently without query, accept as the norm in modern life. So here is the chance for the driver to sit back and be driven, thus affording the opportunity to enjoy the ever-changing scene without the danger of running off the road.

Isle of Skye and Portree (*Highland Omnibus*). A day tour which leaves Fort William every Tuesday at 08.30. It takes you by Glen Shiel and the Five Sisters of Kintail to the Kyle of Lochalsh and then across that very short stretch of water to 'The Winged Isle', the romantic Isle of Skye with the majestic Cuillins. The tour gives you 1½ hrs in Portree.

Inverness and the Culloden Battlefield (*Highland Omnibus*). A day tour which takes you via the Great Glen close by the Caledonian Canal and by the shores of Loch Ness to Inverness and then to the Culloden Battlefield. There is a 2¼ hr break in Inverness with shorter stops at Fort Augustus (both ways) and Culloden.

Glencoe and Inveraray Castle (*Highland Omnibus*). This is a circular day tour going via Glen Coe and Tyndrum to Inveraray where there is a 2½ hr stay, then returning by the Strath of Appin and Ballachulish.

There are also three shorter afternoon tours by Highland Omnibus to Loch Sunart, Moidart and Glenfinnan; Glencoe; Glen Nevis, Commando Memorial and Achnacarry.

Cruises

There is no doubt in my mind that one of the most satisfactory ways to enjoy the wonderful scenery of this part of Scotland is from a viewpoint on the surface of the water, whether it be from the sea just off the coast or from the middle of either a sea loch or a freshwater loch. From offshore the views along this beautiful rugged coastline are seen in better perspective, and views from the middle of a loch allow you to absorb the majestic beauty of both shores and the mountains beyond from a single vantage point which is nearly impossible to achieve from the roadside on one side of a loch. There are a great many cruises available and whether you take one to the offshore islands or along one of the lochs, the experience will be truly memorable.

Below are given details of some of the main cruises but there are many others available by small cruisers operating locally from resorts situated on the seashore or by the shores of the lochs. There is also the attractive combination of sea cruise and coach tour and the triple combination of train via the scenic Mallaig line, followed by sea cruise and coach trip. From 1984 a cruise will run from Fort William to Oban.

Sound of Sleat and Isle of Skye (*Caledonian MacBrayne – Tel: Mallaig 2403 and British Rail – Tel: Fort William (0397) 3791*) – out of **Mallaig** and **Kyle of Lochalsh**.

Tuesdays and *Thursdays* throughout the summer. Fort William to Mallaig, by train, Mallaig to Kyle of Lochalsh, cruise by motor vessel through the Sound of Sleat, passing the entrance to Loch Nevis and Loch Hourn; ferry to Kyleakin; Kyleakin to Armadale through the 'Garden of Skye'; Armadale to Mallaig by ferry; Mallaig to Fort William by train. The whole trip takes about 10½ hrs.

Portree from Mallaig and Kyle of Lochalsh (*Caledonian MacBrayne*) – out of **Mallaig** and **Kyle of Lochalsh**.

Fridays throughout the summer. Mallaig to Kyle of Lochalsh through the Sound of Sleat and, via Raasay, cruise by motor vessel to Portree with 1¼ hrs ashore at Portree; return via Kyle of Lochalsh to Mallaig. The whole trip takes about 9½ hrs.

Crowlin Islands (*Caledonian MacBrayne*) – out of **Mallaig** and **Kyle of Lochalsh**.

Tuesdays throughout the summer from Fort William, Mallaig and Kyle of Lochalsh. Fort William to Mallaig, by train; Mallaig to Kyle of Lochalsh, cruise by motor vessel; cruise around the three Crowlin Islands, which lie between Scalpay (itself an island off Skye) and the mainland just north of loch Carron; return to Kyle of Lochalsh and Mallaig; Mallaig to Fort William by train. The whole trip from Fort William takes about 10½ hrs, and from Mallaig some 6 hrs.

Fishing boats moored at Kyleakin harbour, Isle of Skye

Loch Duich (*Caledonian MacBrayne*) – out of **Mallaig** and **Kyle of Lochalsh**.

Thursdays throughout the summer from Fort William, Mallaig and the Kyle of Lochalsh. Fort William to Mallaig, by train; Mallaig to Kyle of Lochalsh, cruise by motor vessel; then cruise into the beautiful Loch Duich where you have some fine views of Eilean Donan Castle from the water; returning via Kyle of Lochalsh and Mallaig; Mallaig to Fort William by train. The whole trip from Fort William takes about 10½ hrs and from Mallaig some 6 hrs.

Small Isles (*Caledonian MacBrayne*) – out of **Mallaig**.

Mondays throughout the summer – cruise from Mallaig to Eigg, Rhum and Canna. The trip takes some 6¾ hrs.

Wednesdays throughout the summer – cruise from Mallaig to Eigg, Muck, Rhum and Canna. The trip takes some 7 hrs.

Thursdays throughout the summer from Mallaig to Canna, Rhum and Eigg. The trip takes some 6¼ hrs.

Saturdays throughout the summer from Mallaig to Canna, Rhum, Muck and Eigg. The trip takes some 7 hrs.

Small Isles (*Arisaig Marine Ltd. Tel: Arisaig (06875) 224 or 678*) – out of **Arisaig**.

Mondays, Wednesdays and *Fridays* throughout the summer – cruise from Arisaig to Eigg and Muck with ½ hr stay at Eigg and 1½ hrs at Muck or 4 hrs ashore on Eigg.
Tuesdays throughout the summer – cruise from Arisaig to Eigg and Rhum with ½ hr stay at Eigg and 2 hrs at Rhum or 5 hrs ashore on Eigg.
Thursdays throughout the summer – cruise from Arisaig to Rhum with 2¾ hrs ashore on Rhum.
Saturdays throughout the summer – cruise from Arisaig to Eigg with 2½ hrs ashore on Eigg.
Sundays throughout the summer – cruise from Arisaig to Eigg with 3 hrs ashore on Eigg.
Note: On *Mondays, Thursdays* and *Fridays* there are connecting rail services from Fort William with reduced inclusive charges for rail and cruise (*Tel: British Rail – Fort William (0397) 3791*).
Note: A mail boat visits the islands daily all year, and will take passengers.
Eigg (*Eigg Estate. Tel: Mallaig 82413 or 82423*) – out of **Glenuig**.
Monday to Saturday throughout the summer – cruise from Glenuig to Eigg with 5 hrs ashore on Eigg. A minibus meets the boat and there are several tours around the island. These include visits to Camus Sgiotaig with the 'singing sands' via the old crofting settlement of Cleadale.
Loch Nevis, Rhum and Skye (*Bruce Watt. Tel: Mallaig 2233 or 2320 (night)*) – out of **Mallaig**.
Mondays, Wednesdays and *Fridays* throughout the summer by Loch Nevis, morning and afternoon calling at Inverie in Knoydart and Tarbet in North Morar and stopping to view Seal Island – calls at Inverie only on the morning trip. Time taken – 1½ hrs in the morning and 3½ hrs in the afternoon.
Tuesdays throughout the summer by Loch Nevis daily, viewing Inverie and Tarbet and stopping to view Seal Island. Trip takes some 3½ hrs.
Thursdays throughout the summer to the Isle of Rhum. Overall time of trip is 6 hrs.
Saturdays throughout the summer via the Island of Soay to Loch Scavaig and Loch Coruisk at its head right at the foot of the Cuillins in Skye. The trip takes 6 hrs.
Sundays throughout the summer a cruise on Loch Hourn or Loch Nevis.
Loch Etive – Sailings daily from **Taynuilt**. If you took the diversion south through the beautiful Glen Etive finishing up at the head of Loch Etive which I referred to under Glencoe, you may well be tempted to view this beautiful loch by boat – there is no road along either side of the loch. The return trip to the head of the loch takes some 5¼ hrs and the departure time is 10.45 a.m.

Other Cruises

1. There are local cruises from the pier at **Fort William** (*Tel: Fort William 5282, or Fort William Information Office. Tel: Fort William 3581*). April to October.
2. Cruising from **Glencoe** (*Tel: Ballachulish 318*).
3. Cruising from **Onich** (*Tel: Onich 224*).
4. Cruising from **Glenfinnan** on **Loch Shiel** (*Tel: Salen 260 or Corpach 585*).
5. Cruising from **Loch Aline** (*Tel: Morvern 288 (evenings 234)*).

Hiring

Many visitors arrive in Fort William and Lochaber without any other means of transport than their own two feet which, of course, may be the only transport that the hill walker or mountain climber wishes to use, with perhaps the judicious addition of public transport. But for those who do wish to acquire some other means of transport there are adequate hiring facilities available. The facilities listed here are fairly comprehensive but can never be entirely so and the golden rule is that when you are having a problem contact the local tourist office where the staff will do everything they can to solve it.

Car Hire

Macrae & Dick, Fort William. Tel: 2345.
Ben Car Sales, Caol. Tel: Fort William 2408.
Barclay House, Camaghael. Tel: Fort William 4141.
Ness Motors, Fort William. Tel: 4913.
Westco Motors, Spean Bridge. Tel: Spean Bridge 296.

Bicycle Hire

Glenborrodale and Spean Bridge. Contact Fort William Information Office.

Boat and Cruiser Hire

West Highland Yachts. Tel: Fort William 3350/2567/4130.
Glenachulish Centre. Tel: Ballachulish 379.
Corpach Boat Hire and Chandlers. Tel: Corpach 245.
Dalelia Guest House. Tel: Salen 253.
Great Glen Water Park, Loch Oich. Tel: Invergarry 223.
Leacantuim Farm, Glencoe. Tel: Ballachulish 256.
Camerons Cruisers, Onich. Tel: Onich 224.
Ardtornish Estate, Morvern. Tel: Day – Morvern 288, Evening – Morvern 234.
Linnhe Marine Boating Centre, Lettershuna, Appin. Tel: Appin 401.
Loch Leven Chalets, Onich. Tel: Onich 272.
Moidart Yachts, Dorlin, Acharacle. Tel: Salen 278.
Bruce Watt, The Pier, Mallaig. Tel: Mallaig 2233.

Helicopter

Charter Service available. *Burnthills Aviation Ltd. Tel: Fort William 4182 or Glasgow 041–887 7733.*

Sports and Recreation

Angling

It hardly needs restating that Scotland is renowned as a paradise for the angler who is after salmon and trout. Apart from the variety and choice available to the angler it is not always known that in certain cases excellent trout fishing may be enjoyed on lochs and rivers without incurring any charge at all. Although many salmon beats are costly there are also many which are available to the visitor at a reasonable cost. A glance at the map will show that Lochaber is rich in fishing grounds with the many lochs and rivers within its boundaries. Most of these waters are available to the visiting angler by means of daily tickets. Charges on the whole are very reasonable. The salmon season opens on 1 April and though there are few fish moving at this time the keen angler knows that though the fish are few in number it is usually during these early months that the heaviest fish are landed. The best day ticket waters for the visiting angler are the rivers Spean, Roy and Nevis. For sea trout fishing there are good runs on the River Lochy in July and August and loch fishing for sea trout is first class on Loch Shiel and Loch Morar. There is an abundance of water for the loch trout fisherman and included in those which give good sport are lochs Arkaig, Lundavra and

Trout fishing

to a lesser extent lochs Laggan and Lochy. There is no doubt that with the proverbial little bit of luck and the requisite skill the angler will enjoy his stay in Lochaber.

River Fishing
Permits from *Rod & Gun Shop, High Street, Fort William. Tel: 2656.* (Bait also available from this shop.)
River Aline – permits from *Ardtornish Estate, Morvern. Tel: Morvern 288.*

Sea Angling
Loch Aline, Sound of Mull – *Ardtornish Estate, Morvern. Tel: Morvern 288.* Daily trips from pier. Boats for hire.

Loch Fishing
Sea trout and brown trout lochs in **Morvern** – *Ardtornish Estate, Morvern. Tel: Morvern 288.*
Loch Lundavra – permits from *Lundavra Farm, Fort William. Tel: 2582.*
Loch Arkaig – permits from *Keeper's Cottage, Bunarkaig. Tel: Gairlochy 217.*
Loch Morar – charge per boat. Boats available for hire from *Morar Hotel. Tel: Mallaig 2346.*
Loch Shiel – permits from *Stage House Inn, Glenfinnan – Tel: Kinlocheil 246; Glenfinnan House Hotel – Tel: Kinlocheil 235; Dalelia Farm Guest House, Dalelia – Tel: Salen 253; Loch Shiel Hotel, Acharacle. Tel: Salen 224.*
Loch Oich – *Great Glen Water Park, Fishing and Boats. Tel: Invergarry 223.*
Loch Linnhe – free fishing.
Loch Linnhe – *Lettershuna House, Appin, Argyll. Tel: Appin 227.* Boats and tackle.
Loch Lochy – free fishing.
Loch Leven – free fishing.

Many hotels throughout the region have their own fishing rights and guests may apply for permits to the hotel.

Golf

Although the most ardent 'Lochaberphile' would not maintain that the local golf courses vie with St Andrews, Carnoustie, Troon, Gleneagles and other Scottish courses of international renown, for the lover of golf the courses in Lochaber are good ones and offer a considerable challenge to both the low and high handicap golfer.
Fort William (3 miles north of the town). 18 holes. Day tickets available. (*Tel: 4465.*)
Spean Bridge. 9 holes.
Traigh Golf Course, Arisaig. 9 holes.

Other courses within reach are **Fort Augustus** – 9 holes, **Oban** – 18 holes, and if you venture to Skye there is **Portree** – 9 holes and **Sconser** – 9 holes, and in Mull there is **Tobermory** – 9 holes.

Climbing

The climbs in Lochaber are equal to any in the world with those in Glencoe and the north face of Ben Nevis being the most famous. Glencoe offers year-round climbing with easy access off the road and a full range of climbs from the pure novice to the most advanced. Many of the world's finest climbers served their apprenticeship on the mountains of this area and return at regular intervals to accept their continuing challenge. The accommodation needs of the climber are well catered for in the area ranging from hotels, guest houses and bed and breakfast houses to youth hostels, bunkhouses and a barn, to say nothing of caravan and camping sites.
Glencoe School of Winter Climbing. *Tel: Ballachulish 353.*
Glencoe Mountaineering School.
There are maps published by 'Orion', Glencoe (scale 1:25,000) and Ben Nevis and Glen Nevis (scale 4 inches to the mile) available locally

A challenge for two climbers

which give details of the climbs and much other useful information on this highly specialised recreation.

For professional mountain guides and courses, contact '**Nevis Guides**', Bohuntin, Roy Bridge. Tel: Spean Bridge 356. For detailed information on climbing and climbing equipment, contact **Nevisport Ltd**, High Street, Fort William. Tel: Fort William 4921.

Hill Walking

It must be assumed when talking of hill walking that the walker setting out to explore hill tracks in Lochaber is well aware of the need for suitable equipment. Routes can vary from relatively short, dry, well-trodden footpaths, where perhaps no special clothing is required, to much longer, often quite rough, terrain, where scrambling is necessary. Sometimes there are trackless routes over wet boggy ground, when it is absolutely necessary that the walker protects her or himself against the weather and is suitably equipped with proper footwear, protective clothing, a compass, an appropriate map and adequate food supplies.

One of the most imaginative projects in terms of hill walking in Scotland was the introduction in October 1980 of the **West Highland Way**. This statutory long-distance footpath is a new phenomenon in Scottish hill walking and is different in concept from the more traditional view of the Scottish hill walker having free and open access to the hills and walks of his choosing. However, I have no doubt that this will be a popular walk for many hill walkers. It is the first long-distance path in Scotland, stretching some ninety-five miles from Milngavie north to Fort William.

It really is a very fine walk from the outskirts of Glasgow which varies in character, traversing some of the finest scenery of the lowlands at its beginnings and throughout the central Highlands finishing in Fort William. Large sections of the West Highland Way follow old drove roads by which the Highlanders herded their cattle to the lowlands, and it also embraces sections of the famous eighteenth-century military roads built by General Wade and Major Caulfield which were introduced to the Highlands to help control the Jacobite clans. That part of the Way from Rannoch Moor to Fort William falls in the area covered by this guide book. Anyone who considers undertaking this walk is advised to purchase a copy of the official guide to the West Highland Way which is published by Her Majesty's Stationery Office, Edinburgh and is also available from bookshops. The walk is divided into fourteen separate sections which are accessible by public road at either end and the last three of these sections fall into the Lochaber

Hill walkers need proper footwear

area. These are from Kingshouse to Kinlochleven, Kinlochleven to Lundavra, and Lundavra to Fort William. The section from Kingshouse to Kinlochleven is a walk of some nine miles. It climbs over the Devil's Staircase from Glencoe and descends to Kinlochleven at the head of Loch Leven.

The section from Kinlochleven to Lundavra stretches some seven and a half miles and, after a short ascent from Kinlochleven up the northern slopes bordering Loch Leven, the way joins the old military road built by Major Caulfield as far as Lundavra. The last section from Lundavra to Fort William is about six and a half miles. From Lundavra it branches out from the old military route to Fort William through forestry plantations to the head of the valley behind the settlement of Blarmachfoldach. Then it descends quite steeply into Glen Nevis where it eventually joins up with the public road taking it finally into Fort William. The West Highland Way has been comprehensively signposted throughout its length with the Countryside Commission for Scotland's long-distance footpath symbol, which is a thistle within a hexagon on a dark brown base.

Forest walkers in Glencoe

There is an abundance of hill tracks to explore in this part of Scotland and for those who wish to get off the beaten track and investigate some of the old highways and drove roads I would suggest they invest in a very modest publication called *Scottish Hill Tracks – Vol. 1 – Northern Scotland* by D. G. Moir and published by John Bartholomew & Son, which is available locally either at the Tourist Information Centres or booksellers and although this covers the whole of northern Scotland there are some forty routes described which fall into the area covered by this guide book.

Forest Walks

In recent years the Forestry Commission has developed recreational facilities in its forests to the benefit of the public at large. In most cases there are car parks provided at the entrance to the forest so that one may park and then explore the forest on foot. Most people go to a forest to both picnic and walk and in this respect there are many picnic places laid out with tables and benches and usually with toilets adjacent to the car parks. All the Commission's forest walks are way-marked with colour marker posts or discs. Forest trails usually have an explanatory guide leaflet showing numbered halts and accompanied by explanations concerning features of interest along the route.

There are forest walks at:

Glencoe (Map 1) – Signal Rock and An Torr from the National Trust Visitors Centre and the Lochan Forest Trail from Glencoe village.

Barcaldine (Map 1) – Beinn Lora from Benderloch, Eas na Circe from the car park beside Loch Creran; and Glen Dubh from the car park at Sutherland's Grove near Barcaldine.

Clunes (Map 5) – Glaster along the shores of Loch Lochy to Laggan Locks from Clunes; and Chorrach from Clunes.
Cia-aig (Map 5) – Meall Breac overlooking 'The Dark Mile', returning via the Cia-aig river and the 'Witch's Pool' from the car park at the waterfall.
Erracht (Map 5) – A sheltered walk along Glen Loy from the car park on the road to the north of and near to the mouth of the River Loy.
Strone (Map 5) – A short walk to a viewpoint overlooking Fort William and Glen Nevis from a sign on the road just to the south of the mouth of the River Loy.
Achriabhach (Map 4) – Glen Nevis starting from a point near the head of the glen.
Corrychurrachan (Map 1) – Circular forest route giving views of Loch Linnhe and the Ardgour mountains from the car park by the main road 6 miles south of Fort William.
Inchree (Map 1) – A circular route via a fine waterfall, which falls 120 feet in seven stages, and fine views of the Firth of Lorne; from the wooded car park at Inchree, which is just off the A82 just south of the Corran ferry.
Sunart (Map 2) – Ariundle Trail. Through the Strontian Glen oak woods to old lead-mines; from Ariundle, over one mile north of Strontian.
Note: When walking please remember to follow the Country Code.

Guard against all risk of fire.
Fasten all gates.
Keep dogs under control.
Keep to the paths across farmland.
Avoid damaging fences, hedges and walls.
Leave no litter.
Safeguard water supplies.
Protect wildlife, wild plants and trees.
Go carefully on country roads.

Sailing

Whether you are a dinghy sailor or a cruising enthusiast Lochaber offers one of the most attractive sailing areas in the United Kingdom. The ample facilities to hire have been given (p. 119) but if you are a beginner and wish to acquire more skill and practice in the art then there are a number of excellent Sailing Schools to accommodate you.
Glencoe Sailing Instruction. Tel: Ballachulish 350.
Loch Morar Sailing School. Tel: Mallaig 2164.
Glenachulish Centre, Ballachulish. Tel: Ballachulish 379.
Loch Eil Centre, Corpach. Tel: Corpach 320.
Corpach Chandlers and Sailing School, Corpach. Tel: Corpach 245.
Ardnastang Sailing School, Strontian. Tel: Mallaig 82413.
Achanellan Environmental Study Centre, Loch Shiel Lodge, Acharacle. Tel: (0905) 424947.

Swimming

Fort William Swimming Pool, Belford Road. Tel: Fort William 3886.
Sauna and sunray are also available.

Pony Trekking

A pleasant way of enjoying the countryside.
Roshven Farm, Lochailort. Tel: Lochailort 221.
Great Glen Trekking Centre. Tel: Day – Fort William 3015, Night – Gairlochy 238.
Appin: *Lettershuna House, Appin. Tel: Appin 227.*
Loch Garry: *Garry Gualach Adventure Centre. Tel: Tomdoun 230.*

Skiing

There are excellent facilities for downhill skiing at White Corries in Glencoe. There are two chair-lifts and a number of tows. Skiing lasts from late December until May nor-

Skiing in Scotland

mally, with runs of all grades. Skiing is limited to weekend opening during the winter season with extensions at Christmas, New Year and Easter. For special usage outside these times, Tel: Ballachulish 303. See plans of tows and lifts on inset map on Glencoe map, page 7.

Highland Games and Agricultural Shows

Invergarry Highland Games. Third Saturday in July.
Arisaig Highland Games. Last Wednesday in July.
Fort William Highland Games. Last Saturday in July.
Mallaig Highland Games. First Monday in August.
Caol Highland Games. First Saturday in August.
Strontian Agricultural Show. Second Saturday in August.
Glenfinnan Gathering. Saturday after third Tuesday in August.
Fort William Agricultural Show. Last Saturday in August.

Other Main Annual Events

MAY

The International Scottish Six Days Motor Cycle Trial – First full week in May. This traditional event has been running for over seventy years. Not only has this renowned international event maintained its exceptionally high level in sporting appeal, retaining its challenge to the competitors over the years, it has always been a happy social event. So if you are in the Fort William area at the time of the trial go and marvel at the skill of the competitors who come from many parts of the world to compete in this event.

JUNE

Barmouth to Fort William Three Peaks Yacht Race – Starts from Barmouth usually last week in June. This is a sailing and climbing race which was conceived by Major 'Bill' Tilman of Himalayan and Mt Everest fame. The race starts at Barmouth on the west coast of Wales and the object is to sail to Caernarfon on the north-west coast of Wales near the island of Anglesey where two members of the crew then climb to the summit of Snowdon and run back to the boat. The boat then sails on to Ravenglass in Cumbria with another climb to the top of Scafell Pike and finally a sail to Fort William, an ascent of Ben Nevis and a run back to break the finishing tape on the jetty. The race involves sailing of some 350 miles and running and climbing for another 70 miles including the three peaks totalling over 11,000 feet. The race is sponsored by the *Daily Telegraph* newspaper with coverage on Scottish television networks. The first race was in 1977 and it is now established as an annual event with the mountain times decreasing each year.

JULY

Amateur Melantee Hill Race – Same day as Fort William Highland Games (last Saturday in July).
Amateur Half Nevis Race – Sunday after Fort William Highland Games.

AUGUST

Amateur Cow Hill Race – Monday after Fort William Highland Games.
Glen Nevis River Race – Second Sunday in August.
This race takes place in the foaming waters of the River Nevis which includes a frightening leap over the Lower Falls. Further up the course there are the racing white-water sections with the apt names of 'Leg Breaker' and 'Gurgle'. The object of the race is to slip into the water at the start with an air-inflated craft, mostly an air-bed, and get to the finish as quickly as possible – the fastest times being around 21 mins. John Noakes of the BBC Television 'Blue Peter' team has participated in this exhausting bit of fun when some 100 plus entrants compete against the clock, setting off at 30 sec. intervals.

SEPTEMBER

Ben Nevis Race – First Saturday in September.
This race, run up Britain's grandest and highest mountain, is competed for by up to 400 runners. Nowhere else in these islands can one ascend from sea level to 4,406 feet so readily and nowhere else is subjected to so rapid a change in climate.

The male record over this fourteen-mile course is 1 hr 26 mins. 55 secs. The female record is 1 hr 44 mins 25 secs. Visitors will be entertained by a variety of displays during the afternoon.

A Scottish piper, often seen at Highland Games

Other Things to Do and Places to Visit

Museums

West Highland Museum, Cameron Square, Fort William.
Glencoe Folk Museum, Glencoe.
Folk Museum & Cultural Centre, North of Acharacle. (Map 2)

Crafts

Scottish Crafts Exhibition, Fort William – open Easter until mid-October. For the display and marketing of the work of Scottish craftsmen.

White Corries, Glencoe

The chair-lift opposite Kingshouse Hotel. (*Tel: Ballachulish 303 for times of operation in summer.*)

Woollen Mill

You will be sure to enjoy a visit to the woollen mill at Spean Bridge where one can examine at close quarters their interesting hand looms and see the impressive range of Scottish woollens available.

Places to Visit Outside Lochaber but Within Reach

(showing mileages from Fort William)

Inverness *(68 miles)* There is much of interest to see in 'The Capital of the Highlands', as Inverness is sometimes known, and there are many interesting places to see in the area surrounding the town. In Inverness there is the **museum**, with Jacobite and Highland folk-life relics including Highland costume and tartans, and the remarkable **Eden Court Theatre** which is an 800-seat multi-purpose theatre, conference centre and art gallery on the banks of the River Ness. There is a wide variety of shows and exhibitions throughout the year. Outside the town just six miles to the east is the **Culloden Battlefield**. It was on this field on 16 April 1746 that the Jacobite army under Prince Charles was defeated by the army of George II under the Duke of Cumberland. Among the principal features of interest are the graves of the clans – communal burial places with simple head-stones bearing individual clan names. Thirteen miles to the west of Inverness is **Beauly Priory**, a Valliscaulian monastery dating from the early part of the thirteenth century. It is of interest because of its plan, which represents the earliest form of Cistercian church in Britain. Also at Beauly is the **Highland Craft Point** which is an exhibition centre with craft workshops and an audio-visual show illustrating where, why and by whom the crafts are made.

Drumnadrochit – Loch Ness Monster Exhibition *(53 miles)* This exhibition displays all the evidence related to the monsters of Loch Ness and is situated just one mile from **Urquhart Castle** where many of the sightings of 'Nessy' have been made. The exhibition is open all the year round to the public.

The next six places can be bracketed together as they are all reached by the same road from Fort William.

Newtonmore *(50 miles)* This is the location of the **Clan MacPherson Museum** which contains many relics of the Clan, including the fairy gift known as the Black Charter and the broken fiddle of the free-booting James MacPherson, who was sentenced to death in 1701.

Kingussie *(53 miles)* This is the location of **Am Fasgadh** – the **Highland Folk Museum** – which belongs to the universities of Edinburgh, Glasgow, St Andrew's and Aberdeen.

The title is Gaelic for 'shelter' and it contains a fine collection of objects which were in everyday use in the Highlands in the past. The outside exhibits include representative cottages, a mill from Lewis and farm implements.

Kincraig *(58 miles)* Here one can visit the **Highland Wildlife Park** which supports native animals of Scotland both past and present, including wolves, bears, reindeer, wildcat and European bison.

Aviemore *(66 miles)* This is the centre of the **Cairngorm Skiing Area** and has a leisure, sport and conference centre with a wide range of recreational and entertainment facilities. Here there is a **Clan Tartan Centre**, which as well as being a reference library is an exhibition with an audio-visual display. There is also the **Inshriach Alpine Nursery**, which cultivates a wide selection of Alpine and rock plants.

Carrbridge *(73 miles)* Here you can see **Landmark** which is designed as 'Europe's First Visitor Centre'. It is an exhibition, multi-screen auditorium, bookshop, craftshop, restaurant, and nature trail; it is designed to bring alive the history and natural history of the local countryside. This is open all the year round.

Boat of Garten (*70 miles*) This is now the only place in Scotland where you can see ospreys in the nest. They have been successfully nesting and hatching their eggs in this location since 1959. They nest in the centre of the reserve in a tall pine and visitors can watch them at their eyrie from a special observation post.

Skye (*68 miles to Kyle of Lochalsh or 44 miles to Mallaig*) If you travel to Skye via the Kyle of Lochalsh some eight miles short of the Kyle you will pass **Eilean Donan Castle**, which is dramatically sited at the junction of lochs Duich, Alsh and Long near Dornie. The castle was built in 1230 on the site of a vitrified fort and it has been a stronghold of the Earls of Seaforth for many generations. It is open to the public and its exhibits include relics from the Jacobites and a punch bowl used by Dr Johnson during his visit to Raasay. It contains a MacRae war memorial and is open to the public.

There is a great deal to see and much to do on the Isle of Skye; the high brooding **Cuillins** in the south; **Loch Scavaig** and the awe inspiring landlocked **Loch Coruisk**; the majestic **Dunvegan Castle** at the head of the loch of the same name, stronghold of the MacLeods of Skye; the many reminders of Norse invaders; **Flora MacDonald's** grave; and picturesque **Portree**, the island capital.

Oban (*48 miles*) Oban is beautifully set in a sheltered bay with a backcloth of rolling hills and overlooked by MacCaig's Tower, known locally as MacCaig's Folly. From a distance this looks like a replica of an ancient Greek or Roman structure but was in fact intended to be a great museum; it was abandoned because of lack of funds. Here is one of the gateways to the Western Isles and a suitable jumping-off place for visiting **Mull** with its dramatic mountains rising from the sea in the south, its rugged Glen More vividly described in Robert Louis Stevenson's *Kidnapped* and its tales of Spanish galleons and treasure trove in Tobermory Bay; **Iona**, where Columba landed from Ireland in AD 563 and began spreading Christianity throughout Scotland, with its cathedral and St Columba's tomb; **Staffa**, with its fantastic rock columns and the awesome Fingal's Cave (which inspired Mendelssohn's overture); and **Coll** and **Tiree**, two small islands where the soft Gaelic brogue is still spoken and where time virtually stands still.

While in Oban visits can be arranged to **Caithness Glass** where one can witness hand-made glass blowing and the various processes it goes through to the finished article.

Sea Life Centre, Barcaldine (*38 miles*) This display of marine life is situated on the shores of Loch Creran on the same route to Oban and about ten miles from it. This centre is the most modern and comprehensive marine life display in Britain. It was opened in May 1979. Its display techniques are quite ingenious and most informative. As well as displaying the marine life there is a fish farming display showing how the salmon, turbot and oysters are cultivated. It also has a very attractive picnic area just above the sea-shore close by the centre. It is open from 8.30 a.m. to 8.30 p.m. daily April to October.

Great care has been taken to ensure the accuracy of all information at the date of publication, but facilities, times, etc., may be changed periodically by the establishments concerned and it is wise to check locally.

The spelling of place names is almost entirely based on the Ordnance Survey, but it should be noted that there may be local variations on maps and signposts.

Index

Numbers in *italic* type refer to illustrations